The Great SausageMaker Cookbook

For inquiries contact:

Pasta House
P.O. Box 4120
Carlsbad, CA 92018
1-800-795-2512

TABLE OF CONTENTS

The Great SausageMaker Cookbook

TABLE OF CONTENTS

TABLE OF CONTENTS

TABLE OF CONTENTS

Introduction

INTRODUCTION

For Americans sausage evokes pleasant memories of ball games, picnics, backyard barbecues and just plain people having fun together, enjoying life. From the lowly hot dog or frankfurter to the Italian sausage or salami eaten as the family gathers around the table or to the more sophisticated thoughts of European sausages eaten in special restaurants like Tapas Bars, English Pubs, Greek Tavernas, French Bistros or even Italian Trattorias, the sausage holds a place in our hearts.

HISTORY

Sausages have been around for a long time. Originally, they were made out of necessity as one way of preserving meats without refrigeration. They could be dried and hung in a cool place for months.

References to sausage in literature go back as far as Homer with his references to roasting sausage in the *Odyssey*. The Babylonians devoured sausage 1500 years ago by the ton and both the Greeks and the Italians declare themselves the originators of salami. The Romans took sausage to the next level. They created a wide variety of sausages and then even wrote laws governing preparation and when they could be served. Very popular during the reign of Nero as festival food, sausages were later banned from religious festivals by the early Christian church.

Twisting sausages into links began about the middle of the seventeenth century. At this time English sausages were filled with rabbit and capon. Later sausages could be found filled with mutton or pork and oysters mixed together. Then beef sausages became very popular. It was in the nineteenth century that sausage-making was taken over by factories and away from the individual or small local butcher. Craftsmanship was lost as these factories made massive quantities and sold them all over. It remains pretty much the same today with large companies producing most of the sausages sold around the world. However, we are seeing more specialty sausages prepared and sold by the local groceries and butchers. These sausages have a popular draw because they are fresh and are often made with interesting additions, like apples, sun-dried tomatoes, and fresh herbs. These designer sausages have peaked the interest of the consumer and the home sausage maker.

Practically every country in the world has its own type of sausage. Custom, available local ingredients and climate were great influences in how sausage making developed in different areas. Sausages were most often named for the village, town or city in which they had been created . For example, several of the well-known Italian varieties are Genoa Salami from Genoa, Bologna (or Boloney) from Bologna, and Milano Sausage from Milan. Each area developed its own traditions and tastes for certain types of sausage and certain methods of preservation. The preparation of these sausages evolved from available ingredients and relied on the taste and expertise within a town or community and later became known simply by that area's name.

Climate often dictated the sausage preference and the development of standardized recipes. Preservation necessities were the key. In the northern areas, where it was colder, fresh sausages appeared from the fall through winter. However, in the southern areas with more heat, more often sausages were dried and smoked rather than kept fresh.

In the modern world we've kept all the old traditional sausages whether they were originally developed due to custom, available ingredients or climate. What we are mostly concerned with is taste. They are all great. Now, however, with refrigerators and freezers in most homes, making fresh sausage is an easy choice. You can make it and keep it for a few days or freeze it for several months and still have that fresh-made taste.

WHY MAKE YOUR OWN SAUSAGE

There are many advantages to making your own sausages. First, when homemade they simply taste better and are of course, fresher. Second, you can choose exactly what goes into them. You choose the meat, how much fat, the seasonings, and whether to make an all meat sausage or to use a filler. You can make them as hot as you like or as mild. If you don't care for fennel, you are not at the mercy of the manufacturer with his pat recipe.

Third, homemade sausage is also more economical. You can use leftovers or extend the meat with tasty fillers such as oatmeal, soy beans or even bread crumbs. You can even add vegetables or rice to the sausages you make at home. You are in charge.

Last of all, the fresh sausages you create at home are made without preservatives. Commercially prepared fresh sausages often have preservatives added to them to extend their shelf life. You don't need to add any because a batch of sausage is so easy to make using the Popeil Pasta and Sausage Maker, you can make one in a matter of minutes any time you want fresh sausage. Homemade sausage is made fresh to be eaten fresh. Simply freeze any that won't be consumed within a couple of days to preserve that freshness.

WHAT'S IN SAUSAGE

The main ingredient in sausage is the ground meat – pork, beef, veal, lamb, liver, chicken, turkey, fish, seafood or whatever. With the Popeil Pasta and Sausage Maker you don't have to use only ground meat; small chunks of meat may be used also. Most old recipes used no filler at all. Fillers are often used to increase quantity. You can make more at a lower price. However, fillers are also used as a seasoning or to create texture. Oatmeal, soy bean meal, or bread crumbs used in small quantities enhance the taste and texture of the sausage as well as bulking them up.

Fat is used in varying degrees in sausage making. Pork and beef certainly contain more fat than say, turkey or chicken. Some fat, however, is necessary to the flavor and texture of the sausage. When starting with ground meats the fat is already in place. Just choose the percentage you want by choosing leaner or fattier meats.

Along the same line, be warned that the leaner sausages will have less flavor if not seasoned correctly. For instance, adding chopped apples or sun-dried tomatoes to chicken or turkey sausage creates a flavorful and juicy sausage with much less fat.

Seasonings play a key role in the sausage taste. Some sausages are so full of cayenne you gasp as you eat them. Others are so mild you must savor them for their subtleties. Choose sausage fillings that attract you for their seasoning. If you love basil, try fresh basil sausage for a change or an Italian sausage filled with lots of dry basil. If spice is your thing, try sausages with cayenne or red pepper flakes or fresh chilies added to the meat. If you like a smoky sausage but don't actually want to smoke it, try adding liquid smoke to the meat mixture. Don't add too much, it's very strong.

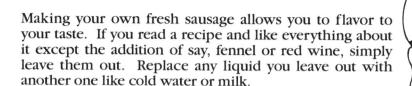

Making your own fresh sausage allows you to flavor to your taste. If you read a recipe and like everything about it except the addition of say, fennel or red wine, simply leave them out. Replace any liquid you leave out with another one like cold water or milk.

Other ingredients you may find in sausage are used for specific reasons to hold the sausage together or hold the color or change the color. Commercial sausages are often made with lots of additives and preservatives. While you don't need the preservatives for your homemade sausages you will often find extra ingredients which seem unnecessary, but serve an important purpose. For instance, milk or dry milk help the sausage keep its color and good looks. Any sugar or honey added to the sausage mixture not only gives a sweet taste but also helps brown the sausage if it is fried or grilled. Eggs act to bind the ingredients together. Salt is used both for flavor and to help in preservation. Don't eliminate the salt, but you may cut down the quantity by half in any recipe.

SAUSAGE-MAKING TIPS

Your Popeil Pasta and Sausage Maker has been designed to be easy to use and clean. Follow any of the over 100 recipes for sausage fillings in this book or let your imagination guide you in creating new recipes using your favorite ingredients. Here are a few tips that will help you prepare your homemade fresh sausages with ease:

• Let your machine rest TWO MINUTES between loads and NEVER put more than two pounds of any meat mixture into the mixing bin at one time.

• For the best outcome, if your recipe does not call for liquid, you may add 1/4 cup of liquid per pound of meat to help move spices through the mixture. Depending on

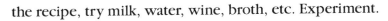

the recipe, try milk, water, wine, broth, etc. Experiment.

• Mix all spices together in a small bowl before sprinkling over the meat mixture. This will insure even mixing.

• Adding a bouillon cube to the meat mixture, dissolved in the recipe's liquid, will enhance the flavor of the sausage, especially the milder chicken and turkey sausages.

• We recommend using 3-1/2 foot lengths of casing. This length is readily accommodated by the sausage cone and is easy to handle as you extrude your sausage.

• Your sausage will taste better if you refrigerate it for 3 to 4 hours before cooking to allow the spices to come to their full flavor.

• Some meat mixtures stick to the sides of the mixing bin and may need to be pushed back into the center of the bin with a rubber or wooden spatula. Be sure to TURN OFF the machine before using the spatula. Switch back to EXT and continue your sausage making.

MAKE CLEANLINESS AND FOOD SAFETY A PRIORITY

Keep the following rules in mind when making fresh sausage:

• Keep meat cool at all times. Work fast, and refrigerate meat as soon as possible. Don't leave meat setting out on the counter if you take a break.

• Sausage links may be refrigerated three to four days before cooking. After that time, wrap well and freeze up

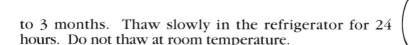

to 3 months. Thaw slowly in the refrigerator for 24 hours. Do not thaw at room temperature.

• Do not taste raw sausage meat. You may smell it or you can form a small patty of the raw mixture and fry it to cook through. Then taste for the balance of spice and seasoning. Make any necessary corrections to the raw mixture.

• When piercing sausage, poke any air bubbles you see. These bubbles are a great place for bacteria to grow.

• Wash your hands thoroughly and often. Remember that bacteria thrives at body temperature.

• Be sure that all surfaces and utensils that come in contact with the sausage as it is being prepared are perfectly clean. This includes cutting boards, knives, spatulas, and all machine parts.

• Keep your working area clear and uncluttered and clean up as you go.

COOKING SAUSAGE

Thorough cooking is absolutely necessary when preparing fresh sausage. Different varieties and different sizes of sausage have different cooking times, but they all should be cooked gently over lower heats. When turning and moving sausage use tongs rather than a fork. Piercing the skin too many times allows the good juices to escape.

Here are several ways to cook sausage:

• **Pan Fry** – Put sausage in a cold skillet with approximately 1/2 cup water and 2 tablespoons vegetable or olive oil. Cook slowly over a medium-low heat for about 10 minutes or until sausage is brown and cooked

through.

• **Broil** – Brush sausage with butter or olive oil and place on a broiler pan. Cook 3 to 4 inches from the heat source, turning often to brown evenly. Watch for burning.

• **Grill** – Brush sausage links with butter or olive oil and grill over low coals very slowly, turning often. The links may also be simmered before grilling to insure that they are cooked all the way through.

• **Bake** – Place sausages on a rack in a shallow baking pan. Cook at 375° for 30 to 45 minutes.

• **Simmer** – Place sausage links in a saucepan large enough to hold them loosely. Cover the sausage with cold water. Place the pan over medium heat and bring the water just to a low simmer. Lower heat and continue to gently simmer for about 10 minutes or until the sausage is cooked through. Do not boil. For fun, try simmering the sausages in beer or wine instead of water.

• **Microwave** – Place sausage links on a microwave-safe grill pan (a bacon rack does nicely) and cook on HIGH power for 5 to 8 minutes depending on number and size of links. Be sure to poke the sausage several times before cooking.

HOW TO SERVE SAUSAGE

Sausages are used throughout the world in stews, soups or salads. They are used to add spice and excitement to all variety of dishes. Rice, potatoes, beans, pasta, and vegetables are vitalized with the addition of sausage. They are often served as the main dish themselves. A bit of mustard, crusty bread, a simple salad and a variety of grilled sausages and dinner is complete.

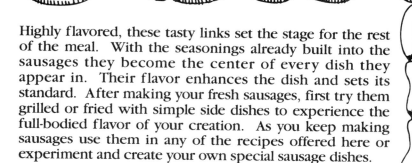

Highly flavored, these tasty links set the stage for the rest of the meal. With the seasonings already built into the sausages they become the center of every dish they appear in. Their flavor enhances the dish and sets its standard. After making your fresh sausages, first try them grilled or fried with simple side dishes to experience the full-bodied flavor of your creation. As you keep making sausages use them in any of the recipes offered here or experiment and create your own special sausage dishes.

SAUSAGE CASINGS AND HORNS

Over the years, sausage casings have evolved from the intestines of hogs and sheep to the collagen and synthetic casings used in most sausages sold today. The edible collagen casings that come with the Popeil Pasta and Sausage Maker provide the perfect finish for your sausage creations. They are easy to use, store easily and come in a variety of sizes.

Standard Sausage Casings and Horns

These 3 horns and a supply of casings come with every machine

#20
Breakfast
1 lb. of meat
mixture makes
about 13
4-inch sausages

#26
Italian
1 lb. of meat
mixture makes
about 10
4-inch sausages

#29
Bratwurst
1 lb. of meat
mixture makes
about 9
4-inch sausages

Additional Sizes

#17
Sm. Breakfast
1 lb. of meat
mixture makes
about 15
4-inch sausages

#32
Lg. Bratwurst
1 lb. of meat
mixture makes
about 8
4-inch sausages

Call 1-800-795-2512 to order
sausage casings, seasonings and more.

Pork Sausages

SAUSAGE CASINGS AND HORNS

The edible collagen casings that come with the Popeil Pasta and Sausage Maker are the best for your sausage creations. They're easy to use, store easily and are available in a variety of sizes.

Standard Sausage Casings and Horns

These 3 horns and a supply of casings come with every machine

#20
Breakfast
1 lb. of meat mixture makes about 13 4-inch sausages

#26
Italian
1 lb. of meat mixture makes about 10 4-inch sausages

#29
Bratwurst
1 lb. of meat mixture makes about 9 4-inch sausages

Additional Sizes

#17
Sm. Breakfast
1 lb. of meat mixture makes about 15 4-inch sausages

#32
Lg. Bratwurst
1 lb. of meat mixture makes about 8 4-inch sausages

Call 1-800-795-2512
to order sausage casings, seasonings and more.

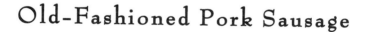

Old-Fashioned Pork Sausage

2 pounds ground pork
1 teaspoon dried thyme
1/8 teaspoon ground nutmeg
Pinch cayenne pepper
Pinch ground ginger
1-1/2 teaspoons salt
1 teaspoon freshly ground black pepper
2 tablespoons cold water

Add pork and remaining ingredients to the mixing bin and process until thoroughly blended. Using the #20 cone extrude the mixture into the casings and twist off into three to four-inch links. Poke several holes down the length of each sausage. Refrigerate and use within three to four days or freeze for later use.

Fresh Sage Breakfast Sausage

2 pounds of ground pork
1/2 cup chopped onion
2 cloves garlic, minced
2 tablespoons minced fresh sage leaves
1 tablespoon minced fresh parsley
2 teaspoons salt
1/4 teaspoon freshly ground black pepper
1/4 cup cream or milk

Add pork and remaining ingredients to the mixing bin and process until thoroughly blended. Using the #20 cone extrude the mixture into the casings and twist off into four-inch links. Poke several holes down the length of each sausage. Refrigerate and use within three to four days or freeze for later use.

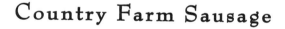

Country Farm Sausage

1/4 pound cold bacon
1-3/4 pounds ground pork
1/2 teaspoon chili powder
1/2 teaspoon marjoram
1/4 teaspoon thyme
1/4 teaspoon ground coriander
2 cloves garlic, minced
1-1/2 teaspoons salt
1/2 teaspoon freshly ground black pepper
1/2 cup cold water

Cut bacon crosswise into one-inch pieces. Process the bacon in the food processor, pulsing until finely chopped. Add chopped bacon, pork and remaining ingredients to the mixing bin and process until thoroughly blended. Using the #20 cone extrude the mixture into the casings and twist off into three to four-inch links. Poke several holes down the length of each sausage. Refrigerate and use within three to four days or freeze for later use.

Hot or Sweet Italian Sausage

Add a teaspoon dried red pepper flakes and a pinch of cayenne pepper to turn these mild sausages into fiery ones.

2 pounds ground pork
2 cloves garlic, minced
1 teaspoon fennel seeds,
slightly crushed (optional)
1 teaspoon dried marjoram
1/2 teaspoon dried oregano
1/2 teaspoon paprika
2 teaspoons salt
1/2 teaspoon freshly ground black pepper
1/3 cup red wine

Add the pork and remaining ingredients to the mixing bin and process until thoroughly blended. Using the #26 cone extrude the mixture into the casings and twist off into four to six-inch links. Poke several holes down the length of each sausage. Refrigerate and use within three to four days or freeze for later use.

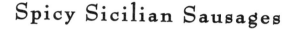

Spicy Sicilian Sausages

These Sicilian sausages rely principally upon fennel seed for their distinctive flavor, but watch out for those red pepper flakes.

2 pounds ground pork or turkey
3 cloves garlic, minced
1-1/2 teaspoons fennel seed, slightly crushed
1 teaspoon crushed red pepper flakes
2 teaspoons salt
2 teaspoons freshly ground black pepper
1/4 cup cold water

Add the pork or turkey and remaining ingredients to the mixing bin and process until thoroughly blended. Using the #26 cone extrude the mixture into the casings and twist off into four to six-inch links. Poke several holes down the length of each sausage. Refrigerate and use within three to four days or freeze for later use.

Fresh Calabrese Salami

These fiery sausages are usually hung to dry for at least eight weeks before sampling. This faster version still yields that traditional flavor from Calabria, the section of Italy well-known for its pork and fiery chilies.

2 pounds ground pork
1 fresh red chili, minced
2 teaspoons crushed red pepper flakes
1/2 teaspoon anise seeds, slightly crushed
1 tablespoon salt
1/4 teaspoon freshly ground white pepper
2 tablespoons dry vermouth
2 tablespoons brandy

Add the pork and remaining ingredients to the mixing bin and process until thoroughly blended. Using the #26 cone extrude the mixture into the casings and twist off into six to eight-inch links. Poke several holes down the length of each sausage. Refrigerate, uncovered, on a rack for 12 to 24 hours. Cover and use within two to three days or freeze for later use.

Italian Citrus Cheese Sausage

2 pounds ground pork
1/2 cup freshly grated Parmesan cheese
1 clove garlic, minced
1/4 teaspoon ground nutmeg
1/4 teaspoon ground coriander
1/4 teaspoon grated lemon zest (rind)
1/4 teaspoon grated orange zest (rind)
1-1/2 teaspoons salt
1/2 teaspoon freshly ground black pepper
1/3 cup dry vermouth

Add the pork, cheese and remaining ingredients to the mixing bin and process until thoroughly blended. Using the #26 horn extrude the mixture into the casings and twist off into four-inch links. Poke several holes down the length of each sausage. Refrigerate and use within three to four days or freeze for later use.

Quick Spaghetti Sausage

Using the dry seasoning mix takes care of the spice and the binding all in one. After browning the sausage in olive oil add to your spaghetti sauce and serve over pasta.

2 pounds ground pork
1/2 cup chopped onion
2 tablespoons chopped fresh parsley
2 tablespoons dry spaghetti sauce mix
1/2 teaspoon salt
1/2 teaspoon freshly ground black pepper
1/4 cup red wine

Add the pork and remaining ingredients to the mixing bin and process until thoroughly blended. Using the #26 horn extrude the mixture into the casings and twist off into four-inch links. Poke several holes down the length of each sausage. Refrigerate and use within three to four days or freeze for later use.

Pizza Pork Sausage

1-1/4 pounds ground pork
1/4 pound pepperoni,
diced in 1/4-inch cubes
1/4 pound mozzarella cheese
diced in 1/4-inch cubes
1 egg, beaten
1-6 ounce can tomato paste
1 teaspoon dried oregano
1/2 teaspoon dried basil
1/4 teaspoon onion powder
1/8 teaspoon garlic powder
1 teaspoon salt
1/4 teaspoon freshly ground black pepper
2 tablespoons milk

Add the pork, pepperoni, cheese and remaining ingredients to the mixing bin and process until thoroughly blended. Using the #26 or #29 horn extrude the mixture into the casings and twist off into four-inch links. Poke several holes down the length of each sausage. Refrigerate and use within three to four days or freeze for later use.

Barbecue Seasoned Sausage

2 pounds ground pork
1/2 cup chopped onion
2 tablespoons minced fresh parsley
1 teaspoon salt
1/2 teaspoon freshly ground black pepper
1/2 cup barbecue sauce

Add the pork and remaining ingredients to the mixing bin and process until thoroughly blended. Using the #26 or #20 horn extrude the mixture into the casings and twist off into four-inch links. Poke several holes down the length of each sausage. Refrigerate and use within three to four days or freeze for later use.

Andouille Cajun Sausage

Andouille sausage is a smoked sausage, but you can achieve a similar flavor in this fresh sausage by adding a bit of liquid smoke. This sausage is great used in gumbos and Jambalaya.

2 pounds ground pork
1 teaspoon sugar
1 teaspoon onion powder
1/2 teaspoon dried thyme
1/4 teaspoon paprika
1/4 teaspoon cayenne pepper
1/4 teaspoon ground allspice
1/8 teaspoon ground nutmeg
1/4 teaspoon liquid smoke (optional)
2 teaspoons salt
1 teaspoon freshly ground black pepper
1/3 cup water

Add the pork and remaining ingredients to the mixing bin and process until thoroughly blended. Using the #26 or #29 horn extrude the mixture into the casings and twist off into four-inch links. Poke several holes down the length of each sausage. Refrigerate, uncovered, for 12 to 24 hours to slightly dry and then use within two days or freeze for later use.

Spicy Creole Sausage

2 pounds ground pork
1/2 cup minced onion
4 cloves garlic, minced
3 tablespoons chopped fresh parsley
1-1/2 teaspoons crushed red pepper flakes
1 teaspoon cayenne pepper
1/2 teaspoon ground allspice
1 teaspoon sugar
2 teaspoons salt
1 teaspoon freshly ground black pepper
1/4 cup cold water

Add the pork and remaining ingredients to the mixing bin and process until thoroughly blended. Using the #26 or #29 horn extrude the mixture into the casings and twist off into four-inch links. Poke several holes down the length of each sausage. Refrigerate and use within three to four days or freeze for later use.

Mexican Chorizo Sausage

1 teaspoon dried chili flakes
3/4 teaspoon paprika
1/2 teaspoon ground coriander
1/2 teaspoon ground cumin
1/2 teaspoon dried oregano
1/4 teaspoon cayenne pepper
1/8 teaspoon ground cinnamon
1/8 teaspoon ground cloves
2 pounds ground pork
1/2 cup chopped onion
2 cloves garlic, minced
2 teaspoons salt
2 tablespoons red wine vinegar

Place the spices and herbs in a small dry skillet over medium-low heat. Cook, tossing often for 3 minutes or until the mixture is quite fragrant. Set aside to cool.

Add the pork, onion, garlic, salt, vinegar and toasted spices to the mixing bin and process until thoroughly blended. Using the #26 horn extrude the mixture into the casings and twist off into two to four-inch links. Poke several holes down the length of each sausage. Refrigerate and use within three to four days or freeze for later use.

Fresh Garlic Sausage

2 pounds ground pork
1/4 cup chopped onion
10 cloves garlic, minced
1/2 teaspoon dried thyme
1/2 teaspoon dried sage
1/2 teaspoon ground ginger
Pinch ground nutmeg
Pinch ground cloves
1 teaspoon salt
1/4 teaspoon freshly ground pepper
1/4 cup cold water

Add pork and remaining ingredients to the mixing bin and process until thoroughly blended. Using the #26 or #20 horn extrude the mixture into the casings and twist off into four-inch links. Poke several holes down the length of each sausage. Refrigerate and use within three to four days or freeze for later use.

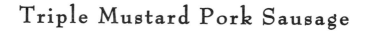

Triple Mustard Pork Sausage

2 pounds ground pork
2 tablespoons minced shallots
2 tablespoons minced fresh parsley
1 tablespoon Dijon mustard
2 teaspoons coarse-grain prepared mustard
1 teaspoon dry mustard
1 teaspoon salt
1/2 teaspoon freshly ground black pepper
1 tablespoon white wine vinegar

Add the pork and remaining ingredients to the mixing bin and process until thoroughly blended. Using the #26 or #20 horn extrude the mixture into the casings and twist off into four-inch links. Poke several holes down the length of each sausage. Refrigerate and use within three to four days or freeze for later use.

Maple Bacon Sausage

These slightly sweet sausages are marvelous served for breakfast or brunch with pancakes or a brunch egg casserole.

1/2 pound maple flavored bacon
1-1/2 pounds ground pork
2 tablespoons real maple syrup
2 tablespoons dark brown sugar
1/2 teaspoon dry mustard
1 teaspoon salt
1/4 teaspoon freshly ground black pepper
2 tablespoons cold water

Cut the bacon crosswise into one-inch pieces. Finely grind in a food processor. Add the bacon, pork and remaining ingredients to the mixing bin and process until thoroughly blended. Using the #20 horn extrude the mixture into the casings and twist off into four-inch links. Poke several holes down the length of each sausage. Refrigerate and use within three to four days or freeze for later use.

Madeira-Mushroom Pork Sausage

2 dried shiitake mushrooms
2 pounds ground pork
1/2 cup coarsely chopped pistachio nuts
2 teaspoons salt
1/4 teaspoon freshly ground black pepper
1/4 cup Brandy
1/4 cup Madeira wine

Place dried mushrooms in a small bowl and cover with hot tap water. Let stand 15 to 20 minutes or until softened. Drain, rinse and chop.

Add pork, mushrooms and remaining ingredients to the mixing bin and process until thoroughly blended. Using the #26 horn extrude the mixture into the casings and twist off into four-inch lengths. Poke several holes down the length of each sausage. Refrigerate and use within three to four days or freeze for later use.

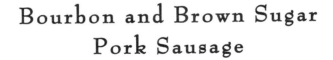

Bourbon and Brown Sugar Pork Sausage

2 pounds ground pork
2 cloves garlic, minced
2 tablespoons dark brown sugar
2 tablespoons soy sauce
1/4 teaspoon dried thyme
1 teaspoon salt
1/2 teaspoon freshly ground black pepper
1/3 cup bourbon

Add the pork and remaining ingredients to the mixing bin and process until thoroughly blended. Using the #26 or #20 horn extrude the mixture into the casings and twist off into four-inch links. Poke several holes down the length of each sausage. Refrigerate and use within three to four days or freeze for later use.

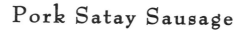

Pork Satay Sausage

Satay is native of both the Philippines and Thailand. There, cubes or strips of meat are skewered and grilled and served with peanut sauce. Here, all the good flavors are mixed together in the sausage itself. Grill and serve with more Thai peanut sauce for dipping.

2 pounds ground pork
1 egg, beaten
1/2 cup chopped onion
2 cloves garlic, minced
3 tablespoons chopped roasted
salted peanuts
1 tablespoon bottled Thai peanut sauce
1 tablespoon fresh lime juice
1 tablespoon soy sauce
1/2 teaspoon hot pepper sauce
1/2 teaspoon salt
1/4 teaspoon white pepper

Add pork and remaining ingredients to the mixing bin and process until thoroughly blended. Using the #26 or #20 horn extrude the mixture into the casings and twist off into two to four-inch links. Poke several holes down the length of each sausage. Refrigerate and use within three to four days or freeze for later use.

Pork and Rice Sausage

Using the rice as a filler in this sausage in no way sacrifices the flavor. What it does is to enhance the texture of this tasty sausage filled with colorful diced vegetables very reminiscent of Chinese Fried Rice.

1 pound ground pork
2 cups cold cooked white rice
2 eggs, beaten and scrambled, then diced
1/4 cup chopped onion
1/4 cup diced red bell pepper
1/4 cup chopped green onion
1 tablespoon minced fresh cilantro
2 tablespoons soy sauce
2 tablespoons dry sherry
1 teaspoon salt
1/2 teaspoon freshly ground white pepper

Add pork, rice and remaining ingredients to the mixing bin and process until thoroughly blended. Using the #29 horn extrude the mixture into the casings and twist off into four to six-inch links. Poke several holes down the length of each sausage. Refrigerate and use within two to three days or freeze for later use.

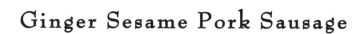

Ginger Sesame Pork Sausage

This exotic oriental-flavored sausage is at its best brushed with teriyaki sauce and grilled.

2 pounds ground pork
1 egg, beaten
2 tablespoons minced fresh ginger
2 cloves garlic, minced
1/4 cup Oriental sesame oil
2 teaspoons soy sauce
2 tablespoons plain dry breadcrumbs

Add pork and remaining ingredients to the mixing bin and process until thoroughly blended. Using the #26 or #20 horn extrude the mixture into the casings and twist off into four-inch links. Poke several holes down the length of each sausage. Refrigerate and use within three to four days or freeze for later use.

Szechuan Sausage

2 pounds ground pork
4 cloves garlic, minced
2 teaspoons sugar
2 teaspoons crushed red pepper flakes
1/2 teaspoon ground ginger
1/4 cup soy sauce
1/4 cup Chinese rice wine or dry sherry
1 teaspoon salt
1/2 teaspoon freshly ground white pepper

Add the pork and remaining ingredients to the mixing bin and process until thoroughly blended. Using the #26 or #20 horn extrude the mixture into the casings and twist off into four-inch links. Poke several holes down the length of each sausage. Refrigerate for one to two days to develop flavor and spice before cooking or freeze for later use.

Greek Pork Sausage With Orange and Red Wine

2 pounds ground pork
3 cloves garlic, minced
2 teaspoons grated orange zest (rind)
1-1/2 teaspoons dried thyme
1 teaspoon dried marjoram
1/2 teaspoon ground allspice
1/2 teaspoon ground coriander
Pinch cayenne pepper
1/3 cup red wine

Add the pork and remaining ingredients to the mixing bin and process until thoroughly blended. Using the #26 horn extrude the mixture into the casings and twist off into four-inch links. Poke several holes down the length of each sausage. Refrigerate and use within three to four days or freeze for later use.

Irish Pork Sausage

1-1/2 pounds ground pork
2 eggs, beaten
3 cloves garlic, minced
1 teaspoon dried thyme
1 teaspoon dried basil
1 teaspoon dried rosemary
1 teaspoon dried marjoram
1-1/2 teaspoons salt
1/2 teaspoon freshly ground black pepper
1-1/2 cups fresh bread crumbs
1/2 cup cold water

Add the pork and remaining ingredients to the mixing bin and process until thoroughly blended. Using the #26 horn extrude the mixture into the casings and twist off into four-inch links. Poke several holes down the length of each sausage. Refrigerate and use within three to four days or freeze for later use.

French Cervelat Sausage

This garlic sausage is slightly dried in the refrigerator and then simmered in a beef broth with the following seasonings: salt, pepper, thyme, basil, bay leaf, parsley and chopped green onions.

1/4 pound bacon
1-3/4 pounds ground pork
3 cloves garlic, minced
1/4 cup minced fresh parsley
2 tablespoons minced green onions
1/2 teaspoon dried thyme
1/2 teaspoon dried basil
2 teaspoons salt
1/4 cup dry white wine

Cut the bacon crosswise into one-inch strips. Finely grind in a food processor. Add the bacon, pork and remaining ingredients to the mixing bin and process until thoroughly blended. Using the #26 horn extrude the mixture into the casings and twist off into four to six-inch links. Poke several holes down the length of each sausage. Refrigerate, uncovered, on a rack for 12 to 24 hours. Refrigerate up to two days longer or freeze for later use.

Braunschweiger

This German sausage is made from pure pork, is mildly spiced and has a distinctive smoky flavor. The pork liver in the recipe lends its own special taste and texture to the sausage.

*1 pound pork liver, trimmed
and finely ground
1 pound ground pork
1 tablespoon finely minced onion
1 tablespoon fresh lemon juice
1 teaspoon sugar
1/4 teaspoon crushed mustard seed
Pinch ground marjoram
Pinch ground allspice
1/8 teaspoon liquid smoke (optional)
1 tablespoon salt
3/4 teaspoon freshly ground white pepper
2 tablespoons nonfat dry milk
1/4 cup cold water*

Add the liver, pork and remaining ingredients to the mixing bin and process until thoroughly blended. Using the #29 horn extrude the mixture into the casings and twist off into six or eight-inch links. Poke several holes down the length of each sausage.

Place sausages in a large pot and cover with water. Heat water just to the point before

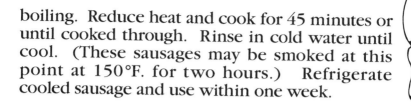

boiling. Reduce heat and cook for 45 minutes or until cooked through. Rinse in cold water until cool. (These sausages may be smoked at this point at 150°F. for two hours.) Refrigerate cooled sausage and use within one week.

Liver Sausage

Liver sausages have a hearty, distinct flavor best brought out by serving with fried onions and mashed or fried potatoes.

1-1/2 pounds boneless pork shoulder
1/2 pound pork or calf liver
8 cups water
1-1/2 teaspoons dried sage
1/4 teaspoon ground allspice
Pinch cayenne pepper
1 tablespoon salt
1/2 teaspoon freshly ground black pepper

Cut pork into two-inch cubes. Place in a 4-quart pot and cover with the water. Bring to a simmer and reduce heat to medium. Cook for about one hour, or until pork is tender. Cut liver into one-inch strips. Add to the pot with the pork and cook for thirty minutes longer, or until the liver is tender.

Drain meats and reserve broth. Cut meats into 1/4-inch cubes and chop in a food processor to a medium fine grind. Strain reserved cooking broth through a fine strainer or cheesecloth. Add one cup broth to the meats and grind again.

Add the meats with broth mixture and remaining ingredients to the mixing bin and process until thoroughly blended. Using the #26 or #29 horn extrude the mixture into the casings and twist off into four to six-inch links. Poke several holes down the length of each sausage.

Immediately put sausage into a deep pot and add water to cover. Bring water to just under a boil. Reduce heat and simmer sausages for 30 minutes or until they float to the surface. Drain sausages, then plunge into cold water to stop cooking. When cool, refrigerate, uncovered, on a rack to dry slightly for 12 hours. Refrigerate, covered, for up to one week longer or freeze for later use.

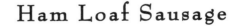

Ham Loaf Sausage

A good old-fashioned dish served up in a tasty new way. Try these served with roasted yam slices and lima beans.

*1-1/2 pounds ground or finely chopped
cooked ham
1/2 pound ground pork
3 shallots, minced
1 egg, beaten
1/4 cup fresh minced parsley
2 tablespoons light brown sugar
1 teaspoon dried thyme
1/2 teaspoon dry mustard
1/2 teaspoon ground nutmeg
1/2 cup milk*

Add meats and remaining ingredients to the mixing bin and process until thoroughly blended. Using the #26 horn extrude the mixture into the casings and twist off into four-inch links. Poke several holes down the length of each sausage. Refrigerate and use within three to four days or freeze for later use.

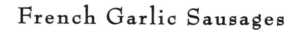

French Garlic Sausages

Very often dried, these fresh sausages are superb grilled and eaten with a simple salad and lots of bread. Just make sure that everyone around you is eating these strong sausages so no one can smell the garlic on anyone else.

2 pounds ground pork
10 cloves garlic, minced
1 tablespoon sugar
1/2 teaspoon paprika
1/2 teaspoon dried oregano
Pinch dried basil
Pinch dried savory or parsley
One pinch each of dried sage, dried thyme,
ground cloves, ground mace,
ground nutmeg, ground cinnamon,
and cayenne pepper
2 teaspoons salt
1 teaspoon freshly ground black pepper
1/4 cup brandy

Add the pork and remaining ingredients to the mixing bin and process until thoroughly blended. Using the #26 horn extrude the mixture into the casings and twist off into four-inch links. Poke several holes down the length of each sausage. Refrigerate, uncovered, on a rack for 12 to 24 hours before grilling. They keep, covered, in the refrigerator another two days before cooking or freeze for later use.

Roasted Red Pepper
Pork Sausage

2 pounds ground pork
1/2 cup diced roasted red pepper
1/4 cup freshly grated Parmesan cheese
1 clove garlic, minced
2 tablespoons chopped fresh basil leaves
1 teaspoon salt
1/4 teaspoon freshly ground black pepper
2 tablespoons cold water or white wine

Add veal and remaining ingredients to the mixing bin and process until thoroughly blended. Using the #26 or #29 horn extrude the mixture into the casings and twist off into four-inch links. Poke several holes down the length of each sausage. Refrigerate and use within three to four days or freeze for later use.

Beef Sausages

SAUSAGE CASINGS
AND HORNS

The edible collagen casings that come with the Popeil Pasta and Sausage Maker are the best for your sausage creations. They're easy to use, store easily and are available in a variety of sizes.

Standard Sausage Casings and Horns

These 3 horns and a supply of casings come with every machine

#20
Breakfast
1 lb. of meat
mixture makes
about 13
4-inch sausages

#26
Italian
1 lb. of meat
mixture makes
about 10
4-inch sausages

#29
Bratwurst
1 lb. of meat
mixture makes
about 9
4-inch sausages

Additional Sizes

#17
Sm. Breakfast
1 lb. of meat
mixture makes
about 15
4-inch sausages

#32
Lg. Bratwurst
1 lb. of meat
mixture makes
about 8
4-inch sausages

Call 1-800-795-2512
to order sausage casings, seasonings and more.

American Beef Sausage

Cut sausages into thin slices and broil slowly until brown on all sides. They are delicious served with French bread slices and a variety of mustards.

2 pounds lean ground beef
1 egg, beaten
2 tablespoons chopped fresh parsley
3/4 teaspoon sage
1/4 teaspoon cayenne pepper
1 teaspoon salt
1/2 teaspoon freshly ground black pepper
1 cup coarse white bread crumbs
1/3 cup water

Add beef and remaining ingredients to the mixing bin and process until thoroughly blended. Using the #29 or #32 horn extrude the mixture into the casings and twist off into six-inch links.

Place sausage into a saucepan and cover with cold water. Bring to a simmer; lower heat and cook gently for 20 to 25 minutes or until cooked through. Remove from pan and allow to cool, then refrigerate and use within three to four days or freeze for later use.

Nacho Cheese Beefy Sausage

1-1/2 pounds ground beef
1/2 pound sharp cheddar cheese, diced in 1/2 inch cubes
1/2 cup chopped onion
2 tablespoons minced fresh parsley
1 tablespoon chili powder
1/4 teaspoon cayenne pepper
1/4 teaspoon ground cumin
1-1/2 teaspoons salt
1/2 teaspoon freshly ground black pepper
2 tablespoons cold water

Add the beef, cheese and remaining ingredients to the mixing bin and process until thoroughly blended. Using the #26 or #29 horn extrude the mixture into the casings and twist off into four-inch links. Poke several holes down the length of each sausage. Refrigerate and use within three to four days or freeze for later use.

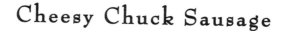

Cheesy Chuck Sausage

Bake, broil or slowly barbecue this delicious beef sausage.

2 pounds ground beef chuck
1-3/4 cups freshly grated Parmesan cheese
4 cloves garlic, minced
1/2 cup minced onion
2 teaspoons dried basil
2 teaspoons dried oregano
1-1/2 teaspoons yellow mustard seed
3/4 teaspoon salt
2 teaspoons freshly ground black pepper
1/2 cup red wine

Add meat and remaining ingredients to the mixing bin and process until thoroughly blended. Using the #29 or #32 horn extrude the mixture into the casings and twist off into four to six-inch links. Poke several holes down the length of each sausage. Refrigerate and use within three to four days or freeze for later use.

Buttermilk Beef Sausage

The addition of the buttermilk adds an unusual tang to this tasty sausage.

2 pounds ground beef
1/2 cup chopped onion
1 tablespoon Worcestershire sauce
1/4 teaspoon ground ginger
1-1/2 teaspoons salt
1/2 teaspoon freshly ground black pepper
1/2 cup buttermilk

Add the beef and remaining ingredients to the mixing bin and process until thoroughly blended. Using the #26 horn extrude the mixture into the casings and twist off into four-inch links. Poke several holes down the length of each sausage. Refrigerate and use within three to four days or freeze for later use.

Blue Cheese Beef Sausage

This recipe is reminiscent of steak with Roquefort sauce and just as satisfying.

2 pounds ground beef
1/4 cup blue cheese salad dressing
3 ounces blue cheese, crumbled
1/4 cup minced onion
1/4 cup minced celery
1/2 teaspoon salt
1/2 teaspoon freshly ground black pepper

Add beef and remaining ingredients to the mixing bin and process until thoroughly blended. Using the #26 horn extrude the mixture into the casings and twist off into four-inch links. Poke several holes down the length of each sausage. Refrigerate and use within three to four days or freeze for later use.

Spicy Beef Sausage

After pan-frying these sausages, slice on an angle and sauté in a mixture of two-to-one butter and hot pepper sauce. It's buffalo wings with an even spicier kick.

2 pounds ground beef
1/4 cup minced onion
3 cloves garlic, minced
1 jalapeno chili, minced
2 tablespoons ketchup
1 tablespoon chili powder
1 teaspoon Dijon mustard
1 teaspoon hot pepper sauce
1/4 teaspoon cayenne pepper
1 teaspoon salt
1/4 teaspoon freshly ground black pepper
2 tablespoons red wine or water

Add beef and remaining ingredients to the mixing bin and process until thoroughly blended. Using the #26 or #29 horn extrude the mixture into the casings and twist off into four-inch links. Poke several holes down the length of each sausage. Refrigerate and use within three to four days or freeze for later use.

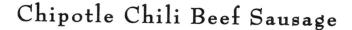

Chipotle Chili Beef Sausage

Chipotle chilies are fresh jalapeños first smoked and then either dried or packed in adobo sauce, a spicy Mexican barbecue sauce. Nothing compares to the smoky spice of these tiny chilies. Be sure not to touch them with ungloved hands, they are very, very hot.

2 pounds ground beef
1/2 cup chopped onion
2 cloves garlic, minced
3 tablespoons minced fresh cilantro
2 canned chipotle chilies in
adobo sauce, minced
1 tablespoon adobo sauce from the chili can
1 teaspoon salt
1/2 teaspoon freshly ground black pepper
2 tablespoons red wine vinegar

Add the beef and remaining ingredients to the mixing bin and process until thoroughly blended. Using the #26 horn extrude the mixture into the casings and twist off into four-inch links. Poke several holes down the length of each sausage. Refrigerate and use within three to four days or freeze for later use.

Beef and Bean Mexican Sausage

1-1/2 pounds ground beef
3/4 cup cooked kidney beans
1/2 cup chopped onion
1/2 cup medium-hot chunky salsa
1 tablespoon Worcestershire sauce
1 tablespoon chili powder
2 teaspoons dry mustard
1-1/2 teaspoons salt
1/2 teaspoon freshly ground black pepper

Add the beef, beans (if using canned beans, rinse well in cold water) and remaining ingredients to the mixing bin and process until thoroughly blended. Using the #26 horn extrude the mixture into the casings and twist off into four to six-inch links. Poke several holes down the length of each sausage. Refrigerate and use within three to four days or freeze for later use.

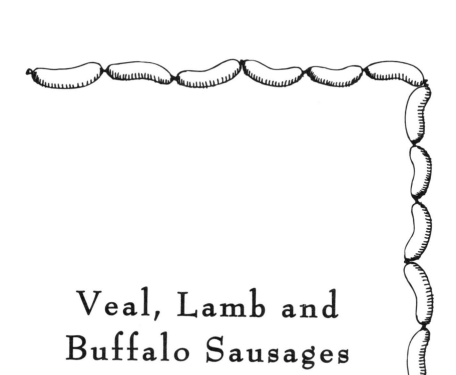

Veal, Lamb and Buffalo Sausages

SAUSAGE CASINGS
AND HORNS

The edible collagen casings that come with the Popeil Pasta and Sausage Maker are the best for your sausage creations. They're easy to use, store easily and are available in a variety of sizes.

<u>Standard Sausage Casings and Horns</u>

These 3 horns and a supply of casings come with every machine

#20 Breakfast
1 lb. of meat mixture makes about 13 4-inch sausages

#26 Italian
1 lb. of meat mixture makes about 10 4-inch sausages

#29 Bratwurst
1 lb. of meat mixture makes about 9 4-inch sausages

<u>Additional Sizes</u>

#17 Sm. Breakfast
1 lb. of meat mixture makes about 15 4-inch sausages

#32 Lg. Bratwurst
1 lb. of meat mixture makes about 8 4-inch sausages

Call 1-800-795-2512
to order sausage casings, seasonings and more.

Golden Veal Lemon Sausage

2 pounds ground veal
2 tablespoons minced shallots
1/2 teaspoon grated lemon zest (rind)
1 teaspoon celery salt
1/2 teaspoon salt
1/2 teaspoon freshly ground white pepper
1/2 cup fresh bread crumbs
1/2 cup milk

Add the veal and remaining ingredients to the mixing bin and process until thoroughly blended. Using the #26 horn extrude the mixture into the casings and twist off into four-inch links. Poke several holes down the length of each sausage. Refrigerate and use within three to four days or freeze for later use.

Minted Lamb Sausage

2 pounds ground lamb
2 cloves garlic, minced
2 tablespoons finely chopped
fresh mint leaves
2 teaspoons finely chopped fresh parsley
1/4 teaspoon grated lemon zest (rind)
1-1/2 teaspoons salt
1/4 teaspoon freshly ground black pepper
1/4 cup plain yogurt

Add lamb and remaining ingredients to the mixing bin and process until thoroughly blended. Using the #26 or #20 horn extrude the mixture into the casings and twist off into four-inch links. Poke several holes down the length of each sausage. Refrigerate and use within three to four days or freeze for later use.

Lamb Sausage with Rosemary

One doesn't ordinarily associate lamb with sausage, but the delicate flavor of true spring lamb can make a delicious sausage.

2 pounds ground lamb
2 teaspoons minced fresh rosemary or 1 teaspoon dried
1 small clove garlic, minced
1 teaspoon salt
1 teaspoon freshly coarse ground black pepper
2 tablespoons dry white wine or water

Add meat and remaining ingredients to the mixing bin and process until thoroughly blended. Using the #26 horn extrude the mixture into the casings and twist off into four-inch links. Poke several holes down the length of each sausage. Refrigerate and use within three to four days or freeze for later use.

Garlic Spinach Lamb Sausage

1-1/2 pounds ground lamb
1 egg, beaten
1-10 ounce package frozen chopped spinach,
thawed and squeezed dry
2 tablespoons chopped fresh parsley
4 cloves garlic, minced
1-1/2 teaspoons salt
1/2 teaspoon freshly ground black pepper
1/4 cup plain yogurt

Add lamb and remaining ingredients to the mixing bin and process until thoroughly blended. Using the #26 horn extrude the mixture into the casings and twist off into four-inch links. Poke several holes down the length of each sausage. Refrigerate and use within three to four days or freeze for later use.

Tomato Curry Lamb Sausage

2 pounds ground lamb
1/2 cup chopped onion
2 teaspoons curry powder
1 teaspoon sugar
1 teaspoon salt
1/2 teaspoon freshly ground black pepper
1/2 cup fresh bread crumbs
1/2 cup tomato sauce

Add the lamb and remaining ingredients to the mixing bin and process until thoroughly blended. Using the #26 or #20 horn extrude the mixture into the casings and twist off into four-inch links. Poke several holes down the length of each sausage. Refrigerate and use within three to four days or freeze for later use.

Apple Curry Lamb Sausage

2 pounds ground lamb
1 egg, beaten
1/2 cup chopped onion
1/3 cup grated peeled apple
2 tablespoons chopped fresh parsley
1/4 cup slivered almonds
1/4 cup chopped mango chutney
1 tablespoon curry powder
2 tablespoons plain dry bread crumbs
2 tablespoons milk

Add the lamb and remaining ingredients to the mixing bin and process until thoroughly blended. Using the #26 horn extrude the mixture into the casings and twist off into four-inch links. Poke several holes down the length of each sausage. Refrigerate and use within three to four days or freeze for later use.

Pickle Relish Lamb Sausage

1-1/2 pounds ground lamb
1 egg white, beaten
1/2 cup chopped onion
1-2 ounce jar pimiento, rinsed and drained
1/2 cup sweet pickle relish
1 teaspoon salt
1/2 teaspoon freshly ground black pepper
1/2 cup fresh bread crumbs
1/2 cup milk

Add the lamb and remaining ingredients to the mixing bin and process until thoroughly blended. Using the #26 horn extrude the mixture into the casings and twist off into four-inch links. Poke several holes down the length of each sausage. Refrigerate and use within three to four days or freeze for later use.

Buffalo Sausage

Ground buffalo is becoming more popular as small herds are being brought back across the West. Buffalo meat is lean and flavorful and can usually be found frozen in specialty meat markets. Try substituting venison for the buffalo in this recipe.

1 cup fresh bread crumbs
1/2 cup milk
1-1/2 pounds ground buffalo
1/2 cup chopped onions
2 cloves garlic, minced
2 tablespoons ketchup
1 tablespoon steak sauce
1 teaspoon dry mustard
1 teaspoon salt
1/2 teaspoon freshly ground black pepper

Soak the bread crumbs in milk for 10 minutes. Add the bread crumb mixture, ground buffalo meat and remaining ingredients to the mixing bin and process until thoroughly blended. Using the #26 or #29 horn extrude the mixture into the casings and twist off into four to six-inch links. Poke several holes down the length of each sausage. Refrigerate and use within three to four days or freeze for later use.

Combination
Sausages

SAUSAGE CASINGS
AND HORNS

The edible collagen casings that come with the Popeil Pasta and Sausage Maker are the best for your sausage creations. They're easy to use, store easily and are available in a variety of sizes.

<u>Standard Sausage Casings and Horns</u>
These 3 horns and a supply of casings come with every machine

#20
Breakfast
1 lb. of meat
mixture makes
about 13
4-inch sausages

#26
Italian
1 lb. of meat
mixture makes
about 10
4-inch sausages

#29
Bratwurst
1 lb. of meat
mixture makes
about 9
4-inch sausages

<u>Additional Sizes</u>

#17
Sm. Breakfast
1 lb. of meat
mixture makes
about 15
4-inch sausages

#32
Lg. Bratwurst
1 lb. of meat
mixture makes
about 8
4-inch sausages

Call 1-800-795-2512
to order sausage casings, seasonings and more.

Bavarian Bockwurst

These mildly seasoned sausages are great served with beer.

1 pound ground pork
1 pound ground veal
1-1/2 tablespoons minced chives
or green onion tops
3/4 teaspoon paprika
1/2 teaspoon ground ginger
1/4 teaspoon ground cardamom
1/4 teaspoon ground nutmeg
1/8 teaspoon ground cinnamon
2 teaspoons salt
1/4 teaspoon pepper
3 tablespoons cream, milk or beer

Add meats and remaining ingredients to the mixing bin and process until thoroughly blended. Using the #29 horn extrude the mixture into the casings and twist off into four to six-inch links. Poke several holes down the length of each sausage. Refrigerate, uncovered, on a rack for 12 to 24 hours to dry slightly before cooking or freeze for later use.

Homemade Kielbasa

Fry these up with lots of fresh onion rings. They are not the usual grocery store hard sausages but the flavor of these fresh homemade sausages is just as pleasing to the palate.

1-1/2 pounds ground pork
1/2 pound ground veal
3 cloves garlic, minced
2 teaspoons dried marjoram
1/4 teaspoon ground allspice
1/8 teaspoon liquid smoke (optional)
2 teaspoons salt
1 teaspoon freshly ground black pepper
2 tablespoons cold water

Add meats and remaining ingredients to the mixing bin and process until thoroughly blended. Using the #26 horn extrude the mixture into the casings and twist off into six-inch links. Poke several holes down the length of each sausage. Refrigerate, uncovered, on a rack for 12 to 24 hours before cooking to dry slightly or freeze for later use.

Bratwurst

These sausages are at their best when simmered slowly in beer to cover. Serve more beer for drinking while you enjoy them with crusty rolls and mustard.

1-1/2 pounds ground pork
1/2 pound ground veal
1/2 teaspoon caraway seeds
1/4 teaspoon dried marjoram
1/8 teaspoon ground allspice
1 teaspoon salt
1/2 teaspoon freshly ground white pepper
1/3 cup cold water

Add meats and remaining ingredients to the mixing bin and process until thoroughly blended. Using the #29 horn extrude the mixture into the casings and twist off into six-inch lengths. Poke several holes down the length of each sausage. Refrigerate and use within three to four days or freeze for later use.

Boudin Blanc

A brightly flavored New Orleans style white sausage made from a combination of ground pork, chicken, fresh bread, eggs and milk or cream.

2/3 cup fresh bread crumbs
1 cup milk or cream
1 pound ground pork
1 pound ground chicken
2 eggs, beaten
1/2 cup chopped onion
3 tablespoons chopped fresh parsley
Pinch ground nutmeg
Pinch ground cloves
Pinch ground cinnamon
Pinch ground ginger
1-1/2 teaspoons salt
1 teaspoon freshly ground white pepper

Toss together bread and milk or cream and let soak for 10 minutes. Add the bread and milk, the pork, chicken and remaining ingredients to the mixing bin and process until thoroughly blended. Using the #26 or #29 horn extrude the mixture into the casings and twist off into four-inch links. Poke several holes down the length of each sausage. Refrigerate and use within three to four days or freeze for later use.

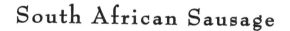

South African Sausage

Though not seen too often because of the warm climate, occasionally these sausages are served hot off the grill.

2 teaspoons ground coriander
1/4 pound bacon
1 pound lean ground beef
3/4 pound ground pork
1/4 teaspoon ground nutmeg
1/4 teaspoon ground cloves
2 teaspoons salt
1/4 teaspoon freshly ground black pepper
1/4 cup cider or white vinegar

Place the coriander in a small skillet over medium-low heat and cook, tossing or stirring constantly, until very fragrant and beginning to smoke. Remove pan from heat immediately and turn coriander out onto a plate to cool.

Cut bacon crosswise into one-inch strips. Place in a food processor and grind very fine. Add the coriander, bacon, pork and remaining ingredients to the mixing bin and process until thoroughly blended. Using the #26 horn extrude the mixture into the casings and twist off into four to five-inch links. Poke several holes down the length of each sausage. Refrigerate and use within three to four days or freeze for later use.

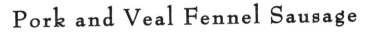

Pork and Veal Fennel Sausage

1 pound ground pork
1 pound ground veal
2 shallots, minced
1-1/2 teaspoons fennel seeds,
crushed slightly in a mortar and pestle
1-1/2 teaspoons dried sage
1/2 teaspoon dried thyme
3/4 teaspoon salt
1/2 teaspoon freshly ground black pepper
3 tablespoons cold water

Add meats and remaining ingredients to the mixing bin and process until thoroughly blended. Using the #26 horn extrude the mixture into the casings and twist off into four-inch links. Poke several holes down the length of each sausage. Refrigerate and use within three to four days or freeze for later use.

Caraway Sausage with Oatmeal

The extension of sausage with grains and bread actually enhances rather than diminishes the flavor. People will never guess that these sausages are not 100% meat unless you tell them. With less meat they are also much leaner.

1 cup quick oatmeal
1/2 cup water
1 pound ground pork
1/2 pound ground veal
1/2 teaspoon caraway seeds
1/8 teaspoon ground allspice
1/8 teaspoon ground ginger
1-1/2 teaspoons salt
1/4 teaspoon freshly ground white pepper

Place oats and water in a small saucepan over medium-high heat and bring to a boil. Drain immediately and cool in the refrigerator for 15 minutes.

Add the cooled oatmeal, pork, veal and remaining ingredients to the mixing bin and process until thoroughly blended. Using the #26 or #29 horn extrude the mixture into the casings and twist off into four to six-inch links. Poke several holes down the length of each sausage. Refrigerate and use within three to four days or freeze for later use.

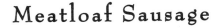

Meatloaf Sausage

Roast these and slice and serve as usual with lots of ketchup and mashed potatoes.

3/4 pound ground beef
3/4 pound ground veal
1/2 pound ground pork
1/2 cup chopped onion
1 egg, beaten
2 tablespoons ketchup
1 tablespoon Worcestershire sauce
2 teaspoons prepared yellow mustard
1-1/2 teaspoons salt
1/2 teaspoon freshly ground pepper
2 slices white bread, cubed and soaked
in 1/2 cup milk

Add meats and remaining ingredients to the mixing bin and process until thoroughly blended. Using the #29 horn extrude the mixture into the casings and twist off into four-inch links. Poke several holes down the length of each sausage. Refrigerate and use within three to four days or freeze for later use.

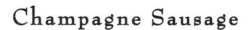

Champagne Sausage

An elegant treat grilled slowly over coals, cut into chunks and dipped into a light mustard sauce.

1 pound ground pork
1 pound lean ground beef
1 large shallot, minced
2 cloves garlic, minced
1-1/2 teaspoons minced fresh marjoram or
1/2 teaspoon dried
1/2 teaspoon paprika
1/8 teaspoon ground cloves
2 teaspoons salt
1/4 teaspoon pepper
1/3 cup champagne

Add meats and remaining ingredients to the mixing bin and process until thoroughly blended. Using the #26 or #29 horn extrude the mixture into the casings and twist off into four-inch links. Poke several holes down the length of each sausage. Refrigerate and use within three to four days or freeze for later use.

Balsamic Italian Sausage

Balsamic vinegar is aged just like wine in barrels for at least 4 years and sometimes up to as much as forty years. This aging creates a smooth rich taste with very little acid.

1 pound ground pork
1 pound ground turkey
1/2 cup chopped onion
2 cloves garlic, minced
1 teaspoon sugar
1 teaspoon dried basil
1/4 teaspoon dried oregano
1/4 teaspoon dried marjoram
1 teaspoon salt
1/2 teaspoon freshly ground black pepper
2 tablespoons seasoned dry bread crumbs
3 tablespoons Balsamic vinegar

Add the pork, turkey and remaining ingredients to the mixing bin and process until thoroughly blended. Using the #26 or #20 horn extrude the mixture into the casings and twist off into four-inch links. Poke several holes down the length of each sausage. Refrigerate and use within three to four days or freeze for later use.

Chutney Raisin Sausage

1-1/2 pounds ground turkey
1/2 pound ground pork
1 egg, beaten
2 tablespoons minced onion
1/3 cup raisins
1/4 cup mango or peach chutney
1 tablespoon soy sauce
1 teaspoon Dijon mustard
3 tablespoons plain dry bread crumbs

Add the turkey, pork and remaining ingredients to the mixing bin and process until thoroughly blended. Using the #26 or #29 horn extrude the mixture into the casings and twist off into four-inch links. Poke several holes down the length of each sausage. Refrigerate and use within three to four days or freeze for later use.

Chicken and Ham Sausage with Horseradish

1 pound ground chicken
3/4 pound ham, finely ground
1 egg, beaten
1/2 cup diced celery
1/4 cup chopped onion
2 tablespoons minced fresh parsley
1/4 cup chopped pimiento stuffed olives
1 tablespoon prepared horseradish
1 tablespoon Worcestershire sauce
1/2 teaspoon salt
1/4 teaspoon freshly ground black pepper
2 tablespoons cold water

Add the chicken, ham and remaining ingredients to the mixing bin and process until thoroughly blended. Using the #26 horn extrude the mixture into the casings and twist off into four-inch links. Poke several holes down the length of each sausage. Refrigerate and use within three to four days or freeze for later use.

Thai Chicken and Turkey
Sausage

1 pound ground turkey
1 pound ground chicken
1 tablespoon minced garlic
1 tablespoon minced fresh ginger
2 tablespoons Southeast Asian fish sauce*
1 teaspoon Southeast Asian hot sauce
(Sriacha Sauce)*
1/2 teaspoon red pepper flakes
2 teaspoons salt
2 teaspoons freshly ground white pepper
2 tablespoons cold water

Add turkey, chicken and remaining ingredients to the mixing bin and process until thoroughly blended. Using the #26 horn extrude the mixture into the casings and twist off into four-inch links. Poke several holes down the length of each sausage. Refrigerate and use within three to four days or freeze for later use.

*These Southeast Asian ingredients are often found in the Oriental section of the grocery store and are always available from an Asian store.

Thai Green Curry Chicken and Turkey Sausage

Thai curry pastes are available in some grocery stores in the Oriental section and always at the Asian stores. These pastes are a fragrant and very spicy blend of chilies, lemongrass, galanga, sugar, cilantro, fish sauce and many other familiar and exotic ingredients.

1 pound ground turkey
1 pound ground chicken
2 cloves garlic, minced
1 teaspoon minced fresh ginger
1/4 cup minced fresh cilantro
1 tablespoon minced fresh basil
1 tablespoon minced fresh mint
1 tablespoon Thai green curry paste
1-1/2 tablespoons Asian fish sauce
1/4 teaspoon crushed red pepper flakes
1 teaspoon salt
1 teaspoon freshly ground white pepper
2 tablespoons cold water

Add the turkey, chicken and remaining ingredients to the mixing bin and process until thoroughly blended. Using the #26 horn extrude the mixture into the casings and twist off into four-inch links. Poke several holes down the length of each sausage. Refrigerate and use within three to four days or freeze for later use.

Spicy Louisiana Sausage

1-1/2 cups sliced onions
1/4 pound bacon
1 pound ground turkey
3/4 pound ground chicken
1 tablespoon chopped garlic
3 tablespoons paprika
2 teaspoons dried thyme
1 teaspoon dried sage
1 teaspoon dried oregano
1 teaspoon sugar
1/2 teaspoon red pepper flakes
1/2 teaspoon dry mustard
1/4 teaspoon cayenne pepper
1/8 teaspoon ground allspice
2 teaspoons salt
1/2 teaspoon freshly ground black pepper

Simmer the onions in water to cover until translucent, 5 to 7 minutes. Cool under cold running water and drain. When completely cool, slice bacon crosswise in one-inch pieces and grind with onions in food processor. Add ground turkey, chicken, bacon and onion mixture and remaining ingredients to the mixing bin and process until thoroughly blended. Using the #26 or #29 horn extrude the mixture into the casings and twist off into four-inch links. Poke several holes down the length of each sausage. Refrigerate and use within three to four days or freeze for later use.

Southwest Green Chili Poultry Sausage

1 pound ground turkey
1 pound ground chicken
1-4 oz. can diced green chilies
1/4 cup chopped fresh cilantro
1 teaspoon minced jalapeño chili
2 tablespoons pure
New Mexican ground chili
1-1/2 teaspoons ground cumin
1/4 teaspoon cayenne pepper
Pinch cinnamon
2 teaspoons salt
1/2 teaspoon freshly ground black pepper
1/4 cup beer

Add chicken, turkey and remaining ingredients to the mixing bin and process until thoroughly blended. Using the #26 horn extrude the mixture into the casings and twist off into four-inch links. Poke several holes down the length of each sausage. Refrigerate and use within three to four days or freeze for later use.

Chinese Roasted Duck Sausage

One 3-pound roasted duckling, meat and skin
removed and coarsely ground
1 slice bacon, ground with duck
3/4 pound ground chicken
2 tablespoons minced fresh cilantro
2 tablespoons minced green onions
2 tablespoons minced waterchestnuts
1 tablespoon minced garlic
1 tablespoon Hoisin Sauce*
2 teaspoons sugar
1 teaspoon Oyster sauce*
Pinch cayenne pepper
1/2 teaspoon salt

Add the ground duck, bacon, and chicken and remaining ingredients to the mixing bin and process until thoroughly blended. Using the #26 horn extrude the mixture into the casings and twist off into four-inch links. Poke several holes down the length of each sausage. Refrigerate and use within three to four days or freeze for later use.

*These Chinese sauces are available in most grocery stores in the Oriental section and in all Asian stores.

Asian Pork and Shrimp Sausage

This mixture is very similar to the one spread on toast and fried, then served as *dim sum*. Pan-fry these sausages and serve with a ginger-soy dipping sauce.

1 pound ground pork
1 egg, beaten
2 teaspoons minced fresh ginger
1 clove garlic, minced
2 tablespoons minced fresh cilantro
1 tablespoon soy sauce
1/4 teaspoon Oriental sesame oil
1 teaspoon salt
1/2 teaspoon freshly ground white pepper
1 pound raw shrimp, peeled,
deveined and chopped

Add the pork and remaining ingredients, except the shrimp, to the mixing bin and process until thoroughly blended. Add the shrimp and process another 20 seconds. Using the #26 horn extrude the mixture into the casings and twist off into four-inch links. Poke several holes down the length of each sausage. Refrigerate and use within two days or freeze for later use.

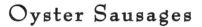

Oyster Sausages

These sausages were popular in both England and New England in the seventeenth, eighteenth and nineteenth centuries when oysters were a lot cheaper than meat. There were many variations of oyster sausages. Some were made only from oysters, others included veal or mutton. These are best pan-fried in butter and then braised, covered, in water until quite done.

2 cups chopped raw oysters
1 pound ground veal
1/4 teaspoon freshly grated nutmeg
2 teaspoons salt
1 teaspoon freshly ground white pepper
1/2 cup plain dry bread crumbs

Cut the oysters into small pieces and place in a food processor. Process as finely as possible. Add the oysters, veal and remaining ingredients to the mixing bin and process until thoroughly blended. Using the #20 horn extrude the mixture into the casings and twist off into four-inch links. Poke several holes down the length of each sausage. Refrigerate and use within three to four days or freeze for later use.

Turkey Sausages

SAUSAGE CASINGS
AND HORNS

The edible collagen casings that come with the Popeil Pasta and Sausage Maker are the best for your sausage creations. They're easy to use, store easily and are available in a variety of sizes.

Standard Sausage Casings
and Horns
**These 3 horns and a supply of casings
come with every machine**

#20
Breakfast
1 lb. of meat
mixture makes
about 13
4-inch sausages

#26
Italian
1 lb. of meat
mixture makes
about 10
4-inch sausages

#29
Bratwurst
1 lb. of meat
mixture makes
about 9
4-inch sausages

Additional Sizes

#17
Sm. Breakfast
1 lb. of meat
mixture makes
about 15
4-inch sausages

#32
Lg. Bratwurst
1 lb. of meat
mixture makes
about 8
4-inch sausages

Call 1-800-795-2512
to order sausage casings,
seasonings and more.

Hot or Sweet Italian Turkey Sausage

Add 1 teaspoon dried red pepper flakes and a pinch of cayenne pepper to turn these mild sausages into fiery ones.

2 pounds ground turkey
2 cloves garlic, minced
1 teaspoon fennel seeds,
slightly crushed (optional)
1 teaspoon dried marjoram
1/2 teaspoon dried basil
1/2 teaspoon dried oregano
1/2 teaspoon paprika
1/4 teaspoon onion powder
2 teaspoons salt
1/2 teaspoon freshly ground black pepper
1/3 cup dry vermouth

Add the turkey and remaining ingredients to the mixing bin and process until thoroughly blended. Using the #26 horn extrude the mixture into the casings and twist off into four to six-inch links. Poke several holes down the length of each sausage. Refrigerate and use within three to four days or freeze for later use.

Italian Turkey Sausage with Sun-Dried Tomatoes

The addition of sun-dried tomatoes to these sausages gives them an attractive look and enhances the flavor three-fold. Grill them and serve in crispy Italian rolls with garlic mayonnaise.

2 pounds ground turkey
2 cloves garlic, minced
1/4 cup minced oil-packed
sun-dried tomatoes
2 tablespoons minced fresh parsley
1/2 teaspoon dried marjoram
1/2 teaspoon dried basil
1/2 teaspoon dried oregano
1/8 teaspoon onion powder
2 teaspoons salt
1/2 teaspoon freshly ground black pepper
2 tablespoons dry vermouth

Add the turkey and remaining ingredients to the mixing bin and process until thoroughly blended. Using the #26 horn extrude the mixture into the casings and twist off into four to six-inch links. Poke several holes down the length of each sausage. Refrigerate and use within three to four days or freeze for later use.

Roasted Red Pepper Basil Turkey Sausage

2 red bell peppers
1-1/2 pounds ground turkey
2 egg whites, beaten
1/2 cup minced onion
3 tablespoons minced fresh basil
1/3 cup ketchup
1 tablespoon soy sauce
2 teaspoons Dijon mustard
1-1/2 teaspoons salt
1/2 teaspoon freshly ground white pepper
1-1/2 cups fresh bread crumbs

Cut the red peppers into quarters and remove the stem and seeds. Lay the pieces flat with skin side up on a large sheet of aluminum foil set on a baking sheet. Press the peppers, if necessary, so they lay flat. Broil until the skin is blackened and bubbly. Remove from broiler, wrap in the foil and let stand 10 minutes or longer to steam. Peel off skin and let cool completely. Dice into 1/2-inch pieces.

Add the turkey, roasted red pepper and remaining ingredients to the mixing bin and process until thoroughly blended. Using the #26 horn extrude the mixture into the casings and twist off into four-inch links. Poke several holes down the length of each sausage. Refrigerate and use within three to four days or freeze for later use.

Roasted Garlic Green Peppercorn Turkey Sausage

The roasted garlic in this recipe is also great spread on toast or added to mashed potatoes along with the milk and butter.

1 head garlic
1 teaspoon olive oil
2 tablespoons green peppercorns packed in brine, rinsed
1-1/4 pounds ground turkey
2 egg whites, beaten
1/2 cup minced onion
1/3 cup ketchup
1 tablespoon soy sauce
2 teaspoons Dijon mustard
1-1/2 teaspoons salt
1-1/2 cups fresh bread crumbs
1/2 cup milk

Remove the loose leaves from the outside of the garlic head, making sure the head remains intact. Trim off the top to expose the garlic cloves. Place the garlic on a piece of aluminum foil and drizzle the cut surface with the olive oil.

Wrap the head and bake at 375°F. for 45 minutes or until the garlic is very soft. Cool garlic completely and then squeeze the soft pulp out of the cloves.

Mash the green peppercorns in a mortar and pestle or with the back of a spoon. Add the turkey, roasted garlic, green peppercorns and remaining ingredients to the mixing bin and process until thoroughly blended.

Using the #26 horn extrude the mixture into the casings and twist off into four inch links. Poke several holes down the length of each sausage. Refrigerate and use within three to four days or freeze for later use.

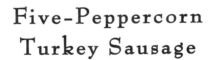

Five-Peppercorn Turkey Sausage

The five-peppercorn blend is made from two types of black peppercorns, white, green and pink peppercorns. The pink ones are actually another type of seed, not really peppercorns at all, but they provide a nice color and interesting flavor. This blend works well in your grinder for everyday use, adding more flavor and less harshness than the plain black varieties.

2 pounds ground turkey
3 tablespoons minced shallots
2 tablespoons minced fresh parsley
2 teaspoons salt
1 tablespoon freshly ground
5-peppercorn blend
1/3 cup dry white wine

Add the turkey and remaining ingredients to the mixing bin and process until thoroughly blended. Using the #20 horn extrude the mixture into the casings and twist off into four-inch links. Poke several holes down the length of each sausage. Refrigerate and use within three to four days or freeze for later use.

Easy Cajun Spice
Turkey Sausage

2 pounds ground turkey
1/2 cup chopped onion
2 tablespoons chopped fresh parsley
2 tablespoons Cajun/Creole spice blend
with no salt
1 teaspoon salt
1/2 teaspoon freshly ground black pepper
1/4 cup cold water

Add the turkey and remaining ingredients to the mixing bin and process until thoroughly blended. Using the #26 horn extrude the mixture into the casings and twist off into four-inch links. Poke several holes down the length of each sausage. Refrigerate and use within three to four days or freeze for later use.

Tex-Mex Sweet Turkey Sausage

2 pounds ground turkey
1/2 cup chopped onion
3 cloves garlic, minced
2 tablespoons minced fresh cilantro
1 serrano chili, minced
2 tablespoons prepared medium salsa
2 tablespoons brown sugar
2 teaspoons dry mustard
1/4 teaspoon cayenne pepper
1 teaspoon salt
1/2 teaspoon freshly ground black pepper
3 tablespoons red wine vinegar

Add the turkey and remaining ingredients to the mixing bin and process until thoroughly blended. Using the #26 or #20 horn extrude the mixture into the casings and twist off into four-inch links. Poke several holes down the length of each sausage. Refrigerate and use within three to four days or freeze for later use.

Pistachio Turkey Sausage

2 pounds ground turkey
1/2 cup coarsely chopped pistachio nuts
1 teaspoon dried sage
Pinch ground allspice
Pinch cayenne pepper
1 teaspoon salt
3/4 teaspoon freshly ground five-peppercorn mix
2 tablespoons cream or milk

Add turkey and remaining ingredients to the mixing bin and process until thoroughly blended. Using the #26 or #20 horn extrude the mixture into the casings and twist off into four-inch links. Poke several holes down the length of each sausage. Refrigerate and use within three to four days or freeze for later use.

Turkey Meatloaf Sausage

Leaner than regular meatloaf but just as tasty.

2 pounds ground turkey
1 egg, beaten
1/4 cup chopped onion
3 tablespoons ketchup
1 tablespoon steak sauce
1 teaspoon salt
1/4 teaspoon freshly ground pepper
1/4 cup seasoned bread crumbs
2 tablespoons cream or milk

Add turkey and remaining ingredients to the mixing bin and process until thoroughly blended. Using the #26 or #29 horn extrude the mixture into the casings and twist off into four-inch links. Poke several holes down the length of each sausage. Refrigerate and use within three to four days or freeze for later use.

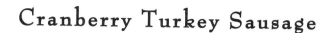

Cranberry Turkey Sausage

Around the holidays this makes a tasty main dish or try serving cut into chunks and dipped into cranberry chutney as an appetizer.

2 pounds ground turkey
1/4 cup chopped onion
2 cloves garlic, minced
1 egg, beaten
1 teaspoon Dijon mustard
1/4 cup whole cranberry sauce
2 tablespoons cold water or white wine

Add turkey and remaining ingredients to the mixing bin and process until thoroughly blended. Using the #26 or #20 horn extrude the mixture into the casings and twist off into four-inch links. Poke several holes down the length of each sausage. Refrigerate and use within three to four days or freeze for later use.

Curried Turkey Sausage

All the best of curry is added to this simple full-bodied lean sausage. Serve with chutney on the side.

2 pounds ground turkey
1/4 cup chopped onion
1 clove garlic, minced
1/4 cup chopped green onions
1/2 cup dark raisins
1/4 cup mango chutney,
with large pieces chopped
2 teaspoons curry powder
Pinch cayenne pepper
1-1/2 teaspoons salt
1/2 teaspoon freshly ground white pepper
2 tablespoons cold water

Add turkey and remaining ingredients to the mixing bin and process until thoroughly blended. Using the #26 horn extrude the mixture into the casings and twist off into four to six-inch links. Poke several holes down the length of each sausage. Refrigerate and use within three to four days or freeze for later use.

Sweet Greek Turkey Sausage with Orange

2 pounds ground turkey
1 clove garlic, minced
1 teaspoon grated orange zest (rind)
1-1/2 teaspoons sugar
1 teaspoon ground cinnamon
1 teaspoon ground allspice
1 teaspoon salt
1 teaspoon freshly ground black pepper
1/3 cup dry white wine

Add the turkey and remaining ingredients to the mixing bin and process until thoroughly blended. Using the #20 horn extrude the mixture into the casings and twist off into four-inch links. Poke several holes down the length of each sausage. Refrigerate and use within three to four days or freeze for later use.

Sweet-Sour Turkey Sausage

These sausages are great served in a sweet-sour sauce with stir-fried vegetables over rice.

2 pounds ground turkey
1 egg, beaten
1/4 cup minced onion
3 cloves garlic, minced
2 tablespoons ketchup
2 tablespoons dark brown sugar
2 tablespoons cider vinegar
2 tablespoons soy sauce
1 teaspoon Dijon mustard
2 tablespoons plain dry bread crumbs

Add turkey and remaining ingredients to the mixing bin and process until thoroughly blended. Using the #26 horn extrude the mixture into the casings and twist off into four-inch links. Poke several holes down the length of each sausage. Refrigerate and use within three to four days or freeze for later use.

Teriyaki Turkey Sausage

2 pounds ground turkey
1/4 cup minced onion
2 cloves garlic, minced
1 tablespoon minced fresh ginger
2 tablespoons Hoisin sauce*
2 tablespoons honey
1 tablespoon soy sauce
2 tablespoons plain dry bread crumbs
2 tablespoons cold water

Add turkey and remaining ingredients to the mixing bin and process until thoroughly blended. Using the #26 horn extrude the mixture into the casings and twist off into four-inch links. Poke several holes down the length of each sausage. Refrigerate and use within three to four days or freeze for later use.

*Hoisin sauce is a special Chinese sauce similiar to barbecue sauce. It can be found in most grocery stores in the Oriental section and at all Asian markets.

Chicken Sausages

SAUSAGE CASINGS
AND HORNS

The edible collagen casings that come with the Popeil Pasta and Sausage Maker are the best for your sausage creations. They're easy to use, store easily and are available in a variety of sizes.

Standard Sausage Casings and Horns

These 3 horns and a supply of casings come with every machine

#20
Breakfast
1 lb. of meat
mixture makes
about 13
4-inch sausages

#26
Italian
1 lb. of meat
mixture makes
about 10
4-inch sausages

#29
Bratwurst
1 lb. of meat
mixture makes
about 9
4-inch sausages

Additional Sizes

#17
Sm. Breakfast
1 lb. of meat
mixture makes
about 15
4-inch sausages

#32
Lg. Bratwurst
1 lb. of meat
mixture makes
about 8
4-inch sausages

Call 1-800-795-2512
to order sausage casings,
seasonings and more.

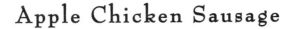

Apple Chicken Sausage

Light and lean, this is truly the sausage of the 90's. Best grilled over mesquite and served in large French rolls topped with lots of dressed mixed greens.

3/4 cup apple cider or juice
2 pounds ground chicken
2 ounces dried apples, chopped
1-1/2 teaspoons dried sage
1/8 teaspoon ground cinnamon
1/8 teaspoon ground nutmeg
1/8 teaspoon ground ginger
2 teaspoons salt
1/2 teaspoon freshly ground black pepper
1 chicken bouillon cube dissolved in 2
tablespoons boiling water

In a small saucepan, boil down the cider almost to a syrup, about 1 to 2 tablespoons. Cool and reserve.

Add the apple cider and the remaining ingredients to the ground chicken in the mixing bin and process until thoroughly blended. Using the #26 horn extrude the mixture into the casings and twist off into six-inch links. Poke several holes down the length of each sausage. Refrigerate and use within three to four days or freeze for later use.

119

Apple Gorgonzola Chicken Sausage

2 pounds ground chicken
1 large tart green apple, peeled,
cored and grated
2 cloves garlic, minced
1/2 teaspoon dried thyme
1/2 teaspoon dried sage
1/2 teaspoon ground ginger
Pinch ground nutmeg
Pinch ground cloves
Pinch cayenne pepper
1/2 teaspoon salt
1/2 teaspoon freshly ground pepper
4 ounces Gorgonzola cheese, crumbled
2 tablespoons cold water

Add chicken and remaining ingredients to the mixing bin and process until thoroughly blended. Using the #26 horn extrude the mixture into the casings and twist off into four-inch links. Poke several holes down the length of each sausage. Refrigerate and use within three to four days or freeze for later use.

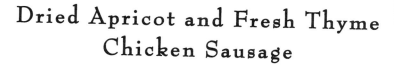

Dried Apricot and Fresh Thyme Chicken Sausage

The addition of fruit and fresh herbs makes this sausage the perfect candidate for grilling and serving with an apricot sauce for dipping.

2 pounds ground chicken
1/4 cup minced dried apricots
2 tablespoons minced shallots
2 teaspoons minced fresh thyme
1 teaspoon sugar
Pinch cayenne
1 teaspoon salt
1/4 teaspoon freshly ground white pepper
2 tablespoons dry white wine or cold water

Add lamb and remaining ingredients to the mixing bin and process until thoroughly blended. Using the #20 horn extrude the mixture into the casings and twist off into two to four-inch links. Poke several holes down the length of each sausage. Refrigerate and use within three to four days or freeze for later use.

Cheesy Chicken Sausage

2 pounds ground chicken
1/4 cup minced onion
2 cloves garlic, minced
1/4 cup ricotta cheese
1/4 cup freshly grated Parmesan cheese
1/4 cup grated Fontina or Muenster cheese
2 teaspoons minced fresh basil
2 teaspoons minced fresh parsley
1 chicken bouillon cube, dissolved in 2
tablespoons hot water

Add chicken, cheeses and remaining ingredients to the mixing bin and process until thoroughly blended. Using the #26 horn extrude the mixture into the casings and twist off into four-inch links. Poke several holes down the length of each sausage. Refrigerate and use within three to four days or freeze for later use.

Fresh Parsley, Sage, Rosemary and Thyme Chicken Sausage

Play the old Simon and Garfunkel song in the background while you serve these sausages and see if your guests catch on.

2 pounds ground chicken
1 egg, beaten
2 tablespoons minced shallots
2 tablespoons minced fresh parsley
1 tablespoon minced fresh sage
2 teaspoons minced fresh rosemary
2 teaspoons minced fresh thyme
1 tablespoon fresh lemon juice
1 teaspoon salt
1/2 teaspoon freshly ground white pepper
1 chicken bouillon cube dissolved
in 2 tablespoons hot water

Add the chicken and remaining ingredients to the mixing bin and process until thoroughly blended. Using the #26 horn extrude the mixture into the casings and twist off into four to six-inch links. Poke several holes down the length of each sausage. Refrigerate and use within three to four days or freeze for later use.

Romano Chicken Sausage

This sausage name comes from that classic trio of Roman flavorings: onions, sweet peppers and freshly grated Romano cheese. To cook, sauté in olive oil until evenly browned and cooked through.

2 pounds ground chicken
1/2 cup finely chopped onion
1/4 cup diced green bell pepper
1/4 cup diced red bell pepper
1/4 cup freshly grated Romano cheese
1 teaspoon dried basil
1 teaspoon salt
1 teaspoon freshly ground black pepper
2 tablespoons cream or milk
or dry white wine

Add chicken and remaining ingredients to the mixing bin and process until thoroughly blended. Using the #26 horn extrude the mixture into the casings and twist off into four-inch links. Poke several holes down the length of each sausage. Refrigerate and use within three to four days or freeze for later use.

Chicken Pesto Sausage

2 pounds ground chicken
1 egg, beaten
1/3 cup prepared basil pesto
2 tablespoons seasoned bread crumbs
1 teaspoon salt
1/2 teaspoon freshly ground white pepper
2 tablespoons dry white wine

Add chicken and remaining ingredients to the mixing bin and process until thoroughly blended. Using the #26 or #20 horn extrude the mixture into the casings and twist off into four-inch links. Poke several holes down the length of each sausage. Refrigerate and use within three to four days or freeze for later use.

Easy Chicken Fajita Sausage

2 pounds ground chicken
1/4 cup chopped onion
1/4 cup diced red bell pepper
1/4 cup diced green bell pepper
1 tablespoon chopped fresh cilantro
2 tablespoons dry Fajita seasoning mix
1/4 cup beer or cold water

Add chicken and remaining ingredients to the mixing bin and process until thoroughly blended. Using the #26 or #20 horn extrude the mixture into the casings and twist off into four-inch links. Poke several holes down the length of each sausage. Refrigerate and use within three to four days or freeze for later use.

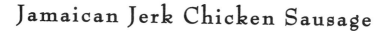

Jamaican Jerk Chicken Sausage

Jerk seasoning was first created in the Caribbean during the slave trade era. The strong seasoning mixture was used to mask the tainted flavor of older, almost spoiled meats. Now, of course, we enjoy it for its spicy flavor and tang.

2 pounds ground chicken
2 shallots, minced
2 cloves garlic, minced
1 serrano chili, minced
1 teaspoon minced fresh ginger
2 tablespoons soy sauce
1 tablespoon honey
1 tablespoon fresh lime juice
1/2 teaspoon ground allspice
1/4 teaspoon ground cloves
1/4 teaspoon ground nutmeg
1 teaspoon salt
1 teaspoon freshly ground black pepper
2 tablespoons dark Rum

Add the chicken and remaining ingredients to the mixing bin and process until thoroughly blended. Using the #26 or #29 horn extrude the mixture into the casings and twist off into four to six-inch links. Poke several holes down the length of each sausage. Refrigerate and use within three to four days or freeze for later use.

Chicken Spinach Sausage

2 pounds ground chicken
1/2 cup cooked, drained chopped spinach
2 cloves garlic, minced
2 tablespoons minced green onions
2 tablespoons minced fresh cilantro
1 teaspoon minced fresh ginger
1 tablespoon soy sauce
1/2 teaspoon Oriental sesame oil
1 chicken bouillon cube dissolved
in 2 tablespoons hot water

Add chicken and remaining ingredients to the mixing bin and process until thoroughly blended. Using the #26 horn extrude the mixture into the casings and twist off into four-inch links. Poke several holes down the length of each sausage. Refrigerate and use within three to four days or freeze for later use.

Fresh Tarragon Smoked Chicken Sausage

1-1/2 pounds ground chicken
1/2 pound smoked chicken or turkey,
diced in 1/4 inch pieces
1 egg, beaten
2 tablespoons minced shallots
3 tablespoons chopped fresh tarragon
2 tablespoons chopped fresh parsley
1/4 teaspoon ground ginger
2 teaspoons salt
1/2 teaspoon freshly ground white pepper
1/4 cup Madeira wine
2 tablespoons cream

Add chicken, smoked chicken or turkey and remaining ingredients to the mixing bin and process until thoroughly blended. Using the #26 horn extrude the mixture into the casings and twist off into four-inch links. Poke several holes down the length of each sausage. Refrigerate and use within three to four days or freeze for later use.

Chicken Brandy Sausage with Fresh Tarragon

2 pounds ground chicken
2 tablespoons minced shallots
1 tablespoon chopped fresh tarragon
1 teaspoon Dijon mustard
Pinch ground nutmeg
1 teaspoon salt
1/4 teaspoon freshly ground pepper
2 tablespoons fresh bread crumbs
3 tablespoons Brandy

Add chicken and remaining ingredients to the mixing bin and process until thoroughly blended. Using the #26 horn extrude the mixture into the casings and twist off into four-inch links. Poke several holes down the length of each sausage. Refrigerate and use within three to four days or freeze for later use.

Fish and Seafood Sausages

SAUSAGE CASINGS AND HORNS

The edible collagen casings that come with the Popeil Pasta and Sausage Maker are the best for your sausage creations. They're easy to use, store easily and are available in a variety of sizes.

Standard Sausage Casings and Horns

These 3 horns and a supply of casings come with every machine

#20
Breakfast
1 lb. of meat
mixture makes
about 13
4-inch sausages

#26
Italian
1 lb. of meat
mixture makes
about 10
4-inch sausages

#29
Bratwurst
1 lb. of meat
mixture makes
about 9
4-inch sausages

Additional Sizes

#17
Sm. Breakfast
1 lb. of meat
mixture makes
about 15
4-inch sausages

#32
Lg. Bratwurst
1 lb. of meat
mixture makes
about 8
4-inch sausages

Call 1-800-795-2512
to order sausage casings, seasonings and more.

Salmon Caper Sausage

2 pounds fresh salmon fillet
2 egg whites, beaten
2 tablespoons capers, rinsed
2 tablespoons minced fresh parsley
2 tablespoons fresh lemon juice
1-1/2 teaspoons salt
1/2 teaspoon freshly ground white pepper

Remove skin and bones from the salmon and cut into cubes. Process the fish in a food processor pulsing just until it is broken up, about three or four on/off cycles. Add the salmon and remaining ingredients to the mixing bin and process until thoroughly blended. Using the #26 horn extrude the mixture into the casings and twist off into four-inch links. Poke several holes down the length of each sausage. Refrigerate and use within two days. These do not freeze well.

Tip: Be sure to rinse the salmon well before processing.

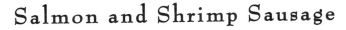

Salmon and Shrimp Sausage

Serve this unusual sausage with a fresh mixed green salad and crispy French bread for a wonderful light lunch.

1-1/2 pounds salmon fillet, cubed
1 egg, beaten
2 tablespoons chopped fresh parsley
1 teaspoon onion powder
1 teaspoon sweet paprika
1 teaspoon lemon juice
1/2 pound raw shrimp, peeled, deveined and chopped into 1/4 inch pieces

Process the salmon in a food processor pulsing just until it is broken up, about three on/off cycles. Add fish and all remaining ingredients except the shrimp to the mixing bin and process until thoroughly blended. Add the shrimp and blend for another 20 seconds. Using the #26 or #20 horn extrude the mixture into the casings and twist off into four-inch links. Poke several holes down the length of each sausage. Refrigerate and use within two days. These do not freeze well.

Tip: Be sure to rinse both the salmon and shrimp well before processing. For faster preparation, try using canned cooked shrimp in place of the raw.

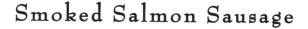

Smoked Salmon Sausage

Grill, slice and serve with bagels and cream cheese for a variation on the traditional.

5 ounces dry smoked salmon
1-1/2 pounds mild, firm white fish, cubed
(use halibut, sea bass or orange roughy)
2 egg whites, beaten
1 tablespoon chopped fresh parsley or dill
1 tablespoon fresh lemon juice
1/4 teaspoon freshly ground white pepper
1/2 cup cream

Break salmon into small pieces and set aside. Process white fish in a food processor pulsing just until it is broken up, about three on/off cycles.

Add white fish and the remaining ingredients except the salmon to the mixing bin and process until thoroughly blended. Add the salmon and process another 20 seconds. Using the #26 horn extrude the mixture into the casings and twist off into four-inch links. Poke several holes down the length of each sausage. Refrigerate and use within two days. These do not freeze well.

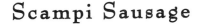

Scampi Sausage

In Italian scampi means shrimp. In this country, however, the term usually refers to a dish made with lots of garlic and butter.

1 pound mild firm white fish, cubed (use halibut, sea bass, or orange roughy)
2 eggs, beaten
1 tablespoon butter, melted
1 tablespoon minced garlic
1 tablespoon minced fresh parsley
1 tablespoon fresh lemon juice
1 teaspoon onion powder
1/2 teaspoon ground allspice
1/4 teaspoon freshly ground white pepper
1 pound raw shrimp, peeled, deveined and chopped

Process the fish in a food processor pulsing just until it is broken up, about three on/off cycles. Add the fish and remaining ingredients, except the shrimp, to the mixing bin and process until thoroughly blended. Add the shrimp and process another 20 seconds. Using the #26 horn extrude the mixture into the casings and twist off into four-inch links. Poke several holes down the length of each sausage. Refrigerate and use within two days. These do not freeze well.

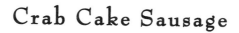

Crab Cake Sausage

Fry these sausages in butter and serve with mayonnaise or be daring and try a spicy roasted red pepper mayonnaise on the side.

1 pound crab meat
1/2 cup regular or low-fat mayonnaise
1 egg, beaten
1/2 cup diced red bell pepper
2 tablespoons minced shallots
1 tablespoon minced fresh parsley
1 tablespoon minced fresh dill
1 tablespoon fresh lemon juice
2 teaspoons Worcestershire sauce
1 teaspoon hot pepper sauce
1 teaspoon dry mustard
1/4 teaspoon paprika
1/4 teaspoon freshly ground black pepper
1-1/2 cups fresh bread crumbs

Pick through the crabmeat and remove any shell or cartilage. Add the crab and remaining ingredients to the mixing bin and process until thoroughly blended. Using the #26 horn extrude the mixture into the casings and twist off into four-inch links. Poke several holes down the length of each sausage. Refrigerate and use within two days. These do not freeze well.

Lobster Sausage

1-1/2 pounds mild firm white fish fillets,
cubed (try halibut, sea bass,
or orange roughy)
1 egg, beaten
1/2 teaspoon ground mustard
1/2 teaspoon ground coriander
1 teaspoon sweet paprika
1 teaspoon fresh lemon juice
1/2 teaspoon freshly ground white pepper
1/2 pound lobster meat, coarsely chopped

Process the fish in a food processor pulsing just until it is broken up, about three on/off cycles. Add fish and all remaining ingredients except the lobster to the bin and process until thoroughly blended. Add the lobster meat and blend for another 20 seconds. Using the #26 horn extrude the mixture into the casings and twist off into four-inch links. Poke several holes down the length of each sausage. Refrigerate and use within two days. These do not freeze well.

Old Bay White Fish Sausage

Old Bay seasoning is a long-standing tradition for seasoning fish and for crab boils. This seasoning blend makes quick work of this sausage.

2 pounds mild firm white fish, cubed (use halibut, sea bass, or orange roughy)
2 egg whites, beaten
2 tablespoons minced shallots
1 tablespoon Old Bay seasoning
1/2 teaspoon salt
1/2 teaspoon freshly ground white pepper
2 tablespoons dry vermouth

Process the fish in a food processor pulsing just until it is broken up, usually three on/off cycles. Add the fish and remaining ingredients to the mixing bin and process until thoroughly blended. Using the #26 or #20 horn extrude the mixture into the casings and twist off into four-inch links. Poke several holes down the length of each sausage. Refrigerate and use within two days. This sausage does not freeze well.

Asian Fish Sausage

1 pound mild firm white fish, cubed
(use halibut, sea bass, or orange roughy)
1 egg, beaten
1/2 cup chopped onion
2 tablespoons chopped fresh cilantro
2 teaspoons minced fresh ginger
1 clove garlic, minced
1 teaspoon minced jalapeño chili
1/4 teaspoon ground tumeric
1/4 teaspoon freshly ground white pepper
1 pound raw shrimp, peeled, deveined
and chopped

Process the fish in a food processor pulsing just until it is broken up, about three on/off cycles. Add white fish and remaining ingredients except the shrimp to the mixing bin and process until thoroughly blended. Add the shrimp and process another 20 seconds. Using the #20 horn extrude the mixture into the casings and twist off into four-inch links. Poke several holes down the length of each sausage. Refrigerate and use within two days. These do not freeze well.

Tuna Sausage

2 12-1/2 ounce cans
chunk light tuna in oil
2 anchovy fillets
1/2 teaspoon finely minced fresh rosemary
or 1/4 teaspoon dried, crumbled
1/2 cup fine dry bread crumbs
1/2 cup freshly grated Parmesan cheese
2 eggs, beaten
1 teaspoon dry mustard
1/8 teaspoon ground nutmeg

Drain tuna and mix in a food processor until very fine, but do not puree completely. Add tuna mixture and remaining ingredients to the mixing bin and process until thoroughly blended. Using the #26 or #20 horn extrude the mixture into the casings and twist off into four-inch links. Poke several holes down the length of each sausage. Refrigerate and use within three to four days or freeze for later use.

Tuna Salad Sausage

If you love tuna sandwiches and tuna casseroles, why not try these. They're great served cold at a picnic or tailgate party.

two 12-1/2 ounce cans
chunk light tuna in oil
3/4 cup regular or low-fat mayonnaise
1 egg, beaten
1/2 cup diced celery
2 tablespoons chopped fresh parsley
1 tablespoon fresh lemon juice
2 teaspoons Dijon mustard
1 tablespoon Worcestershire sauce
1/4 teaspoon hot pepper sauce
1/2 teaspoon salt
1/4 teaspoon freshly ground white pepper
2/3 cup fresh bread crumbs

Drain tuna and mix in a food processor until very fine, but do not puree completely. Add tuna and remaining ingredients to the mixing bin and process until thoroughly blended. Using the #26 horn extrude the mixture into the casings and twist off into four-inch links. Poke several holes down the length of each sausage. Refrigerate and use within three days. These do not freeze well.

Breakfast

SAUSAGE CASINGS
AND HORNS

The edible collagen casings that come with the Popeil Pasta and Sausage Maker are the best for your sausage creations. They're easy to use, store easily and are available in a variety of sizes.

Standard Sausage Casings and Horns

These 3 horns and a supply of casings come with every machine

#20
Breakfast
1 lb. of meat
mixture makes
about 13
4-inch sausages

#26
Italian
1 lb. of meat
mixture makes
about 10
4-inch sausages

#29
Bratwurst
1 lb. of meat
mixture makes
about 9
4-inch sausages

Additional Sizes

#17
Sm. Breakfast
1 lb. of meat
mixture makes
about 15
4-inch sausages

#32
Lg. Bratwurst
1 lb. of meat
mixture makes
about 8
4-inch sausages

Call 1-800-795-2512
to order sausage casings,
seasonings and more.

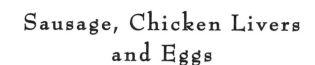

Sausage, Chicken Livers and Eggs

Use only the freshest chicken livers in this recipe and you'll be rewarded with the most exquisite flavor.

1/2 pound chutney raisin sausage (page 89)
1 tablespoon butter
1/2 pound fresh chicken livers, rinsed, dried, and coarsely chopped
1 tablespoon chopped fresh chives
8 eggs, well beaten
salt and freshly ground black pepper to taste

Sauté the sausage until it is brown, about ten minutes. Remove it with a slotted spoon, cut into bite-sized pieces and set aside. Discard the drippings. Add the butter to the skillet and sauté the chopped chicken livers four or five minutes. Return the sausage to the skillet. Add chives and eggs, add salt and pepper to taste. Stir constantly over medium heat until the eggs are fluffy and well scrambled.

Serves 4

Sausage Quiche

Try dividing the mixed ingredients for a quiche and making small individual servings to use as an appetizer by using small tart shells instead of a pie plate. Dieters be warned: this dish is absolutely guaranteed to blow any diet—past, present or future!

For the pastry:

1 cup sifted flour
1/4 teaspoon salt
1/3 cup vegetable shortening
4 tablespoons (approximately) cold water

Sift the flour together with the salt. Cut the shortening into marble-sized pieces and mix it into the flour with a pastry blender. Sprinkle the water on a little at a time while mixing continuously with the pastry blender. Make the dough into a ball. Roll the pastry out into a circle large enough to cover a nine-inch pie plate with the edges overlapping. Line the pie plate with the pastry and trim the edges.

For the filling:

1/2 pound balsamic
Italian sausage (page 88)
1/2 pound fresh mushrooms, sliced

1 small onion, chopped
1/2 small sweet green pepper,
cored, seeded, and chopped
3 eggs, well beaten
2 cups half and half
4 ounces mozzarella or
Gruyere cheese, shredded
1/4 cup Romano cheese, grated
Dash of cayenne pepper
salt to taste
freshly ground black pepper (optional)

Sauté the sausage in a skillet until it loses its pink color. Remove it with a slotted spoon and set it aside. In the sausage drippings, sauté the mushrooms, onions, and peppers until they are crisp-tender. Remove them with a slotted spoon and set them aside. Discard the drippings. Beat the eggs, and while you continue to beat, add the half and half, cayenne pepper, salt, and pepper. Put the sausage into the pastry shell. Layer the onion, mushroom, and pepper mixture evenly over the sausage. Spread the grated cheeses over all. Finally, pour the egg and cream mixture over everything. Bake in a preheated 400°F. oven for about thirty minutes. Allow the quiche to cool for about ten minutes before slicing. Note: to make individual quiches, simply divide the pastry and ingredients among as many tart shells as you plan to use.

Serves 4 as an entree. Serves 6-10 as an appetizer.

Scrambled Eggs and Sausage

A breakfast classic that is best made in a double boiler. Expand it for as many people as you have to serve.

1/4 pound hot or sweet Italian
turkey sausage (page 101)
2 eggs, well beaten
2 tablespoons heavy cream
1/2 teaspoon freshly snipped parsley, chopped
salt, freshly ground black pepper
and basil to taste

Cook sausage under the broiler or in a frying pan, whichever is your favorite method. While they are browning, break at least two eggs for each person you will be serving, and put them in a bowl. Bring the double boiler to a simmer. Whisk the eggs, add cream, parsley, salt, pepper and basil to taste.

Rub the top of the double boiler with butter. Add the eggs and cook for about two minutes. Uncover them and begin working with the whisk again, cook for five more minutes. For harder scrambled eggs cook 1-2 minutes longer. Take the sausages from the broiler or the skillet and halve them. Add them to the eggs and serve with a tomato slice.

Serves 1

Country-Style Sausage and Eggs

If there is anything more versatile than sausage it would probably have to be the egg. Here's a simple recipe for one serving using both. Expand it for as many people as you have to serve.

1/4 pound country farm sausage (page 27)
2 eggs, well beaten
1 tablespoon milk
1 teaspoon freshly snipped chives
1 tablespoon grated Parmesan cheese
salt and freshly ground black pepper to taste

Cut sausages into bite-sized pieces. Sauté the sausage until it is browned, about ten minutes. Drain off most of the grease. In a mixing bowl combine the eggs, milk, chives, cheese, salt and pepper. Mix well. Over medium heat, pour the scrambled egg mixture into the skillet with the sausage, stirring constantly until the eggs are set.

Serves 1

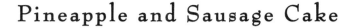

Pineapple and Sausage Cake

Pineapple and sausage? Why certainly. This recipe is so simple that it can be made in minutes. This dish gets served with a garnishing of parsley or chopped chives, fresh or frozen. It makes a fine breakfast or lunch.

*1 pound Old Fashioned
pork sausage (page 25)
2 eggs, well beaten
1-1/2 cups milk
2 tablespoons melted butter
or vegetable oil
2 cups sifted all-purpose flour
3 teaspoons baking powder
pinch of salt
1 16-ounce can pineapple slices
horseradish or mustard to taste*

Brown the sausages in a large skillet. Drain off the excess grease. Remove from heat, cut into lengthwise slices and keep warm.

For pancakes, mix together the eggs, milk, and butter or oil in a mixing bowl. Sift in the flour, baking powder, and salt. Use a whisk to beat the mixture until it is smooth and free of lumps

Make the pancakes in a lightly oiled griddle and set aside. Drain a can of sliced pineapple and rub

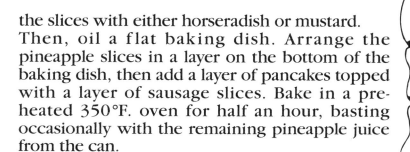

the slices with either horseradish or mustard. Then, oil a flat baking dish. Arrange the pineapple slices in a layer on the bottom of the baking dish, then add a layer of pancakes topped with a layer of sausage slices. Bake in a pre-heated 350°F. oven for half an hour, basting occasionally with the remaining pineapple juice from the can.

Serves 4

Sausage and Mushroom Omelet

Of all the things you can do with eggs the omelet has to be one of the most perfect. And yet many people shy away from making omelets because they think that they are difficult. Making a perfect omelet only takes a little more patience and effort than perfectly scrambling an egg. Fillings for omelets are limited only by your taste and imagination.

*1/4 pound madeira-mushroom
sausage (page 41)
2 tablespoons butter
1 tablespoon finely minced onion
1/4 cup chopped fresh mushrooms
2 eggs
2 tablespoons milk
salt to taste
freshly ground black pepper to taste*

In a small skillet or omelet pan sauté the sausage until it is browned. Remove the sausage with a slotted spoon and discard the drippings. Cut into bite-sized pieces and set aside. Melt the butter in the skillet and add the onion and mushrooms. Sauté until the onions are translucent and the mushrooms have given up some of their juice. While the onions and mushrooms are cooking, beat the eggs until they are smooth and frothy. Stir in the milk, salt and pepper.

When the onions and mushrooms are ready, pour the eggs into the pan over them. Cook the omelet over medium heat, tilting the pan and lifting the omelet's edges now and then to allow the uncooked mixture on the surface to flow underneath. When the omelet is almost set sprinkle the sausage on one side and fold the omelet over. Serve immediately. Garnish with parsley if desired.

Serves 1

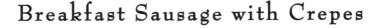

Breakfast Sausage with Crepes

This is a new way to have your pancakes and sausage for breakfast. Use the basic crepe batter recipe on opposite page.

16 crepes (see recipe on opposite page)
1 pound Italian citrus cheese
sausage (page 31)
Maple syrup

Prepare the crepes and keep them warm. Sauté the sausage in a skillet until it is well browned. Remove it with a slotted spoon and keep it warm. Layer the crepes and sausage on individual plates. (Plan on stacking at least three or four crepes per person.) Pass the maple syrup at the table.

Serves 4-6

Crepes

Crepes, or very thin pancakes, are fun food and yet they are very elegant. They can be made in a variety of ways and if you are lucky enough to have an electric crepe maker you're all set. A non-electric crepe pan works just as well and an ordinary skillet will even do.

1 cup cold water
1 cup cold milk
4 eggs
1/2 teaspoon salt
2 cups all-purpose flour
4 tablespoons butter, melted

Put all ingredients in a blender in the order listed. Whirl 1 minute. Scrape down sides and blend another minute. Refrigerate batter at least 2 hours. Heat a 7-inch crepe pan or iron skillet over medium-high heat until very hot. Pour in a scant 1/4 cup batter. Tilt pan in all directions so batter runs evenly over bottom. Pour out any excess batter. Return pan to heat for 1 minute. Turn crepe when bottom is lightly browned. Cook 30 seconds on second side. Slide out of pan onto waxed paper. Repeat with remaining batter.

Makes 16 crepes.

Dagwood Brunch

This is a knife-and-fork sandwich that can be a showcase for several of your homemade sausages. Dagwood Bumstead would be in heaven if he found this dish lying in wait in the back of the refrigerator at three in the morning and so would you.

16 crepes (see recipe on previous page)
1 dozen thin slices each of three
or four different sausages
1 medium onion sliced thinly
1/2 cup sliced stuffed green olives
1/4 cup chopped dill pickle
1/4 cup herbed salad dressing
(see recipe opposite)
6 slices Swiss cheese

Prepare the herbed salad dressing and set aside. Prepare the crepes. Arrange half the crepes on a baking sheet. Layer half the sausages, onion, olive, and pickle on these crepes. Repeat layers with remaining crepes and ingredients. Sprinkle an equal amount of dressing on each crepe sandwich. Top each sandwich with a slice of Swiss cheese and bake in a pre-heated 400°F. oven for about ten minutes or until the cheese is melted.

Serves 6

Herbed Salad Dressing

3 tablespoons of red wine vinegar
1/2 teaspoon sugar
1/2 teaspoon salt
1/4 teaspoon each of oregano,
basil, and thyme
dash of cayenne
freshly ground black pepper to taste
1 tablespoon of olive oil

Add all ingredients to a container that can be tightly sealed and shake vigorously. If you prepare your dressing ahead of time it will allow the herb flavor to develop to its fullest.

Sausage and Apple Pancakes

Sausages and pancakes go together like bread and butter. Make your own pancakes from scratch using the recipe here or use your favorite packaged mix.

1 pound bourbon and brown sugar
pork sausage (page 42)
2 large apples, peeled, cored,
and chopped coarsely
1/2 cup apple jelly
2 eggs, well beaten
1-1/2 cups milk
2 tablespoons melted butter
or vegetable oil
2 cups sifted all-purpose flour
3 teaspoons baking powder

Brown the sausage in a large skillet. Add the apples and cook until tender. Drain off the excess grease and stir in the apple jelly. Remove from heat and keep warm. Mix together the eggs, milk, and butter or oil in a mixing bowl. Sift in the flour, baking powder, and salt. Use a whisk to beat the mixture until it is smooth and free of lumps. Make the pancakes on a lightly oiled griddle. As soon as each one is done, top with a sausage and some of the apple/jelly mixture, then roll up. Serve immediately with maple syrup.

Serves 4

Basic Meals

SAUSAGE CASINGS
AND HORNS

The edible collagen casings that come with the Popeil Pasta and Sausage Maker are the best for your sausage creations. They're easy to use, store easily and are available in a variety of sizes.

Standard Sausage Casings and Horns

These 3 horns and a supply of casings come with every machine

#20
Breakfast
1 lb. of meat
mixture makes
about 13
4-inch sausages

#26
Italian
1 lb. of meat
mixture makes
about 10
4-inch sausages

#29
Bratwurst
1 lb. of meat
mixture makes
about 9
4-inch sausages

Additional Sizes

#17
Sm. Breakfast
1 lb. of meat
mixture makes
about 15
4-inch sausages

#32
Lg. Bratwurst
1 lb. of meat
mixture makes
about 8
4-inch sausages

Call 1-800-795-2512
to order sausage casings, seasonings and more.

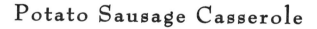

Potato Sausage Casserole

For an added twist try adding more onion and some parsley, as well as about one-half a head of cabbage, pre-boiled with some carraway seeds. Some pieces of dry bread, soaked in water or milk, also go well in this dish.

1 pound loose fresh sage
breakfast sausage (page 26)
5 medium-sized potatoes
1 small onion chopped
1/4 teaspoon oregano
salt to taste
freshly ground black pepper

The sausage should be precooked in about 1/2 cupful of water for about fifteen minutes. Break the sausage with a fork as it cooks. Drain off excess fat. Combine all the other ingredients with the sausage and turn into a 1-1/2 quart casserole. Cover and bake in a 325°F. oven about one hour, or until the potatoes are tender.

Serves 4

Sausage Roll

Try serving a thick slice of this appetizer with a selection of mustards. This dish goes well with a main course like a spicy fish soup, stew, curry, or gumbo.

*1 cup unbleached all-purpose
pre-sifted flour
1/4 teaspoon salt
4 tablespoons unsalted butter,
cut into small pieces
1/4 cup water
1 pound garlic sausage (page 38)
1 egg, lightly beaten with
1 tablespoon water*

To make the dough in the processor: process the flour and salt until well mixed. Add the butter and process until the mixture has the texture of bread crumbs. Pour in the water while the processor is running and stop as soon as the dough is well mixed. If you mix dough by hand, be sure to blend butter evenly throughout the mixture.

Whichever method you use, place the dough on a sheet of waxed paper or plastic wrap and pat into a rectangle. The dough will be soft but not sticky. Wrap it in the paper and refrigerate until you're ready to use it. Prick the sausage in 2 to 3 places with a fork. Place in a saucepan or skillet and pour in water to cover. Bring to a boil, then reduce heat to low and simmer for 10-20 minutes.

Preheat the oven to 350°F. Remove the dough from the refrigerator. Roll it out on a floured board until 1/8" thick. You want the rectangle to be long and wide enough to roll the sausage up completely in the dough. Cut away any excess dough and reserve. Roll up the sausage in the dough, pressing to seal well. Cut out 2 circles from the remaining dough and use to close up the open spaces at the ends of the sausage. Crimp them where they meet the rest of the dough to seal well. Turn the sausage so the seam side of the dough is on the bottom and place on a non-stick baking sheet.

Use the rest of the dough to make decorative cutouts. Attach them with the egg and water mixture, then brush the whole roll with the egg glaze. Bake for 45 minutes until browned all over. The sausage can be served hot or warm, but make sure you cut it with a serrated knife or the dough will get crushed.

Serves 4

Cranberry Sausage Casserole

This casserole is good all by itself, but it can be improved by serving fresh peas or corn on the side, along with some coleslaw or some bread-and-butter pickles. Add some fresh, crusty French or Italian bread for a hearty meal.

2 cups fresh cranberries
1 cup granulated brown sugar
4-5 sweet potatoes
1/2 cup water
2 pounds Greek pork sausage with
orange and red wine (page 47)

Preheat the oven to 350°F. Boil sweet potatoes. Allow them to cool, then peel and slice them and set aside. Wash cranberries. Put the cranberries and granulated brown sugar into a large casserole and mix well. Add water to the cranberry brown sugar mixture, and put the sweet potato slices over the berries. Place sausage links on top. Salt and pepper liberally. Cover and bake for 1-1/2 hours. Remover cover and continue to bake until the sausages are brown all over. Turn them occasionally, if you wish, trying not to prick them. Use a wooden spoon.

Serves 4

Quick, Easy Sausage Stew

For an appealing look garnish with parsley. Serve with plenty of bread for the mop-up procedure and coleslaw on the side.

2 pounds spicy Sicilian sausage, browned
and sliced into 2-inch pieces (page 29)
4-5 potatoes
1 or 2 16-ounce cans kidney beans
(red or white)
salt to taste
freshly ground black pepper

Boil the potatoes and sausage in 1 quart of water until potatoes are soft. Add beans, salt and pepper to taste, heat through and serve.

Serves 4

Pennsylvania Dutch Sausage Pie

One of the best recipes out of the Pennsylvania Dutch country is this one for a pie. For a delightful change experiment with other recipes of sausage.

1-1/2 pounds potatoes cut into chunks
1 pie crust dough recipe for covered pie
12 to 14 1-inch lengths of Italian
citrus cheese sausage (page 31)
fresh parsley
freshly ground black pepper

In salted water, boil the potatoes until almost tender. Sauté sausage lightly in a small skillet and set aside. While the potatoes are cooking take some pie crust dough and line a pie tin with it, reserving some of the dough for the topping. Place sausage lengths into the pie. Sprinkle with parsley and a small pinch of freshly ground black pepper. Layer the potatoes over the sausage. Sprinkle a few drops of water over the mixture before the lid of crust is set on. Bake in 450°F. oven for 20 minutes.

Serves 6

Beef Sausage Casserole

This unsophisticated dish is standard fare in rural areas throughout the country.

2-1/2 cups of dry bread made into cubes
1/2 cup beef broth
2 or 3 small potatoes, diced
1 12-ounce package of frozen peas
1-1/2 pounds of American beef sausage
cut into 1-inch lengths (page 59)

Place bread cubes into a large mixing bowl and mix together with potatoes, peas, and about half of the sausage. Add broth, then put into a greased casserole. Arrange remaining sausage on top of casserole. Bake at 350° for about an hour, or until potatoes are soft. Take the lid off the for the last 15 minutes of baking so the casserole forms a crusty top.

Serves 4–6

Creole Sausage Stew

This spicy stew is best served with fresh garlic bread and a fresh salad. Great for cold winter days.

1 pound spicy Creole sausage (page 36)
1 cup chopped onions
1/2 cup chopped green peppers
2 tablespoons flour
1 29-ounce can tomatoes
2 cups cooked or canned whole-kernel corn
1 bay leaf
1/2 teaspoon thyme
1-1/4 teaspoons salt
Dash Tabasco

Cut each sausage crosswise into 4 pieces; cook until browned in a large skillet. Remove the sausages. Drain all but 2 tablespoons of fat. To the fat remaining add the onions and green peppers; sauté 5 minutes. Blend in the flour. Add the tomatoes, corn, bay leaf, thyme, salt, and Tabasco. Cook over low heat 20 minutes. Return the sausages to skillet and cook 5 minutes longer.

Serves 6

Scalloped Sausage and Potatoes

Tote this to your next pot luck and you'll be the hit of the party.

1 pound maple bacon sausage (page 40)
4 cups thinly sliced potatoes
1/4 cup all-purpose flour
1/4 teaspoon salt
1 cup shredded sharp Cheddar cheese
1-1/2 cups milk

In skillet crumble sausage and brown it lightly; drain thoroughly. Place half of the sliced potatoes in a 2-quart casserole. Combine flour and salt. Sprinkle half the seasoned flour mixture over the potatoes. Top with half the browned sausage and half of the cheese. Repeat layers with remaining potatoes, flour mixture, sausage, and cheese. Pour milk over all. Cover and bake at 350° till potatoes are tender, 50 to 60 minutes. Uncover and bake 10 minutes more.

Serves 4 -6

Kielbasa with Green Beans and Carrots

This dish falls in between a soup and a stew. Plan on having some fresh, crusty rye bread on hand to soak up the delicious juices.

*1 pound homemade kielbasa, cut
into one-inch pieces (page 80)
1 small onion, sliced thinly
1 cup dry white wine
2 cups water
2 cups Italian (Romano) green beans,
cut into one-inch pieces
2 cups carrots, scraped and sliced
1 bay leaf
2 tablespoons chopped parsley
1 teaspoon paprika
salt and freshly ground black pepper*

Put the kielbasa into a heavy pot with just enough water to cover the bottom. Cook over medium heat until the sausage gives up some of its grease and is lightly browned, about ten minutes. Add the onion and cook about five minutes or until the onion is translucent. Add the remaining ingredients and cook for about forty minutes or until the vegetables are tender. Remove the bay leaf. Serve in bowls.

Serves 4

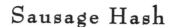

Sausage Hash

The word hash has negative connotations for many people because it conjures up thoughts of leftovers that should have been left to rest. It needn't be so. There is nothing leftover about this recipe (unless of course you make too much).

*1 pound old fashioned pork sausage
removed from the casing (page 25)
1/2 cup chopped onion
4 cups peeled, cooked, and
chopped potatoes
1/2 cup cooked chopped carrots
Hot fat for frying*

Sauté the sausage until it is lightly browned. Sauté the onion in the sausage drippings until it is translucent, about ten minutes. Add the potatoes and carrots to the sausage and mix well. Form the mixture into patties and brown in hot fat.

Serves 4

Texas-Style Sausage Chili

This is real Texas-style chili with lots of kidney beans in a hot, spicy sauce and enough meat to make any Texan brag.

1 pound spicy beef sausage (page 64)
2 cloves garlic, minced
1 medium onion, chopped
3 tablespoons chili powder (or substitute your own combination of spices such as ground chilis, cumin, coriander, fenugreek, and oregano)
1 28-ounce can kidney beans
2 cups tomato puree
salt and freshly ground black pepper to taste

Cut sausages into bite-sized chunks and sauté until lightly browned. Add the garlic and onion and cook ten minutes. Add the chili powder, beans, tomato puree, salt and pepper. Simmer about forty-five minutes or until thickened.

Serves 4

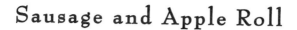

Sausage and Apple Roll

This is a meat roll which bakes up just like a meatloaf.

2 pounds Irish pork sausage
without casing (page 48)
3 apples, peeled, cored, and chopped
1 small onion, coarsely chopped
1-1/2 cups fresh bread crumbs
1/4 teaspoon nutmeg (optional)
1/4 teaspoon ground allspice (optional)
Dash of cayenne (optional)
salt and freshly ground black pepper to taste

On a large piece of waxed butcher paper spread out the sausage in the form of a rectangle about a half an inch thick. In a mixing bowl combine the remaining ingredients. Spread the apple mixture over the sausage rectangle, leaving an inch-wide border all the way around. Roll up the sausage jelly roll fashion. Begin by picking up one end of the waxed paper and folding it over until the roll gets started. The meat should fall away from the paper easily. This helps prevent the sausage from breaking apart. Pinch the ends together to seal. Place the roll in a greased pan and bake in a preheated 375°F. oven for one hour.

Serves 8

Boiled Capon with Sausage Stuffing and Celery Sauce

Rich English families often served two birds at Christmas, one boiled, the other roasted and presented with a garland of sausages around its neck. Even though this dish is boiled, the celery sauce gives it a festive feeling. Accompany the capon with mashed potatoes or potato pancakes and sautéed green vegetables. Try a light red wine, such as a Beaujolais, with the meal.

1 8-pound capon
1 pound Champagne sausage
cut into 1-inch lengths (page 87)
1 bay leaf
3 sprigs fresh thyme, or 1/2 teaspoon
dried & crumbled
3 carrots, roughly chopped
1 onion, halved and stuck with 2 cloves
16 celery stalks with leaves,
each cut into 5 or 6 pieces
2 tablespoons unsalted butter,
room temperature
2 tablespoons white flour
1 cup heavy cream
1/2 teaspoon salt
1/4 teaspoon freshly ground black pepper
1 tablespoon lemon juice

Remove any excess fat and skin and the giblets from the capon. Loosely stuff the capon with the sausage meat, then truss it. Place the capon in a large pot, scatter the giblets, bay leaf, thyme, carrots, and onion around it, then cover it with cold water. Turn the heat to high, bring the water to a boil, then reduce heat to low. Simmer the pot, covered, for 2 hours, adding the celery after 1-1/2 hours.

Just before the capon is finished cooking, knead together the butter and flour to make a roux and set it aside. Remove the capon and all the celery from the stock. Pureé the celery in a food processor or blender. Put the celery pureé and two cups of strained capon stock into a small saucepan and turn heat to low. Bring the pureé just to a simmer, then stir in the roux. Simmer, stirring often, for another 5 minutes. Stir in the cream, salt, and pepper. Simmer for 10 more minutes, stirring often.

While the sauce is simmering for the last 10 minutes, carve the capon. Stir the lemon juice into the sauce and immediately remove it from the heat. Arrange the capon, sausage stuffing, carrots and onions on a large platter and serve with the sauce in a sauceboat on the side.

Serves 8

International

SAUSAGE CASINGS
AND HORNS

The edible collagen casings that come with the Popeil Pasta and Sausage Maker are the best for your sausage creations. They're easy to use, store easily and are available in a variety of sizes.

<u>Standard Sausage Casings and Horns</u>

**These 3 horns and a supply of casings
come with every machine**

#20
Breakfast
1 lb. of meat
mixture makes
about 13
4-inch sausages

#26
Italian
1 lb. of meat
mixture makes
about 10
4-inch sausages

#29
Bratwurst
1 lb. of meat
mixture makes
about 9
4-inch sausages

<u>Additional Sizes</u>

#17
Sm. Breakfast
1 lb. of meat
mixture makes
about 15
4-inch sausages

#32
Lg. Bratwurst
1 lb. of meat
mixture makes
about 8
4-inch sausages

Call 1-800-795-2512
to order sausage casings, seasonings and more.

Sausage Curry

Try sprinkling with 1/4 cup slivered almonds before serving.

2/3 cup long grain rice
2 medium apples, cut in wedges and cored
1 medium onion, cut in wedges
2 tablespoons margarine or butter
1 beef bouillon cube
1 tablespoon cornstarch
1-1/2 teaspoons curry powder
3/4 pound Szechuan sausage, browned
and cut into 1-inch pieces (page 46)
1/2 cup raisins

Prepare rice according to package. In skillet brown apples and onion in margarine; remove and set aside. In the same skillet dissolve bouillon in 1 cup hot water and bring to a boil. Combine cornstarch, curry powder, and 1/4 cup cold water. Add to bouillon, stirring until mixture thickens. Add sausage, onion, and apples. Cook over low heat until apples and onion are tender. Meanwhile cover raisins with water and bring to a boil. Remove from heat and allow to stand for 5 minutes. Drain raisins, then combine with rice and place on a platter. Arrange sausage on top of rice mixture then pour sauce over all.

Serves 4

Pizza Rustica

Pizza rustica is in a sense a misnomer since this dish is anything but rustic. It requires careful attention to detail if you want it to be as pleasing to the eye as it is to the palate. Plan on eight servings for an antipasto or six servings as the main course at a luncheon. With a dry, well-chilled white wine and a tossed green salad this dish could be a complete meal.

1 recipe pie crust dough
1/4 pound spicy beef sausage cut
into 1/2-inch slices (page 64)
2 tablespoons olive oil
1 small onion, chopped
2 cloves garlic, minced
1/4 cup (total) chopped red
and green sweet peppers
1/4 cup pepperoni, diced
1/4 cup hard salami, diced
1 tablespoon black olives, chopped
8 ounces mozzarella cheese, shredded
1/4 cup grated Parmesan cheese
1/4 cup spaghetti sauce
salt
freshly ground black pepper

Prepare the pie crust dough and divide it in half. Roll out one piece and place it in a deep dish nine-inch pie plate. Roll out the other half and reserve it for the top crust. Crumble the sausage in a skillet, add the olive oil, and saute it until the meat loses its pink color, about five or ten minutes. Remove the meat with a slotted spoon and set it aside. In the oil and sausage drippings sauté the onion, garlic, and chopped peppers until they are crisp-tender. Remove them with a slotted spoon. Discard the grease. In a bowl mix together the sausage, pepperoni, salami, onions, peppers, and chopped olives. Add salt and pepper to taste. Spread a thin layer of mozzarella on the bottom crust. Add about a third of the meat mixture and spread it evenly over the cheese. Dot with about a third of the spaghetti sauce and then sprinkle on a third of the Parmesan cheese. Repeat the layering process, ending with a layer of mozzarella cheese. Place the top crust over the filling and press with a fork to seal the edges. Brush the top with cold water and bake in a preheated 350°F. oven for thirty-five minutes or until the top is golden.

Serves 6-8

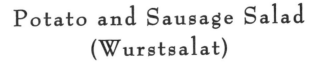

Potato and Sausage Salad (Wurstsalat)

German potato salad makes a nice change from the American mayonnaise-laden version. Cooking the onions in the stock before adding them gets rid of the sharp raw onion taste, but if you like raw onions you can just chop and add them without boiling them first.

6 cups chicken or beef stock, homemade
preferable but canned is acceptable
2 medium onions, halved
salt to taste
1 pound (about 8) small red boiling potatoes
1/2 cup diced celery or celeriac
1/2 cup browned, diced Bratwurst (page 81)
1/4 cup vegetable oil
3 tablespoons wine vinegar
2 teaspoons prepared mustard
(preferably German)
1 tablespoon minced fresh parsley
3/4 teaspoon minced fresh thyme or 3/8
teaspoon crumbled dried
1/8 teaspoon freshly ground black pepper

Bring the stock and onions to a boil over high heat in a large saucepan. Add the salt and potatoes. If there isn't enough stock to cover the potatoes, add more. Once the pot returns to a boil, cook for 20 minutes, until the potatoes are tender. Remove the potatoes with a slotted spoon and peel as soon as you can. (If you tear the skin off in large enough pieces, you can toss the pieces of skin with butter and bake them in a hot oven until crisp for a wonderful snack.) Remove the onion from the stock with a slotted spoon. Halve the peeled potatoes lengthwise, then cut into 1/4"-thick half circles. Return the potatoes to the stock and let them cool to room temperature. Cooling them in the stock lets them absorb a lot of wonderful flavor. When the potatoes and stock are room temperature, remove the potatoes with a slotted spoon and place in a salad bowl with the celery and sausage. Remove the onions with a slotted spoon, finely chop, and add to the bowl. Place the oil, vinegar, mustard, parsley, thyme, pepper, and 2 tablespoons of the stock into a jar, screw on the lid, and shake well. Pour over the potatoes and toss gently, being careful not to crumble the potatoes. Serve warm or at room temperature.

Serves 6

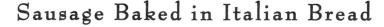

Sausage Baked in Italian Bread

An excellent way to feed a crowd inexpensively and well is to serve this spicy sausage and cheese loaf with a hearty soup, a salad and a very special dessert.

1 large Italian bread
2 medium onions,
peeled and coarsely chopped
3/4 cup minced mushrooms
1 sweet red pepper with seeds,
pith and stem removed
2 tablespoons oil
1-1/2 pounds quick spaghetti
sausage, removed from casing (page 32)
1 clove garlic, peeled and crushed
1/8 teaspoon sage
1/4 teaspoon each oregano and thyme
3/4 cup grated cheddar,
Swiss or jack cheese
1 egg, beaten
1/4 cup heavy cream

Cut the top third of the bread off in one slice. Pull out the soft center portion of the bread, leaving a 1-inch thick shell. Reserve the soft bread pieces you pull out. Sauté the onions, mushrooms and sweet peppers in the oil. Force these sautéed vegetables, the sausage meat, soft bread pieces, garlic, sage, oregano and thyme through a grinder three times. Preheat oven to 350°F. Thoroughly mix the cheese, egg and cream into the meat mixture with a wooden spoon and stuff the bread shell with the mixture. Cover the stuffed bread with the top slice and wrap well in 2 thickness' aluminum foil, set on baking sheet and bake for 1 hour. Open foil and allow loaf to brown during the last 15 minutes.

Serves 4-6

Bigos (Polish Peasant Stew)

Serve with fresh bread and salad.

2 tablespoons butter
1 cup chopped onions
2 pounds boneless pork, cut in l-inch cubes
1 pound French garlic sausage (page 55)
3 cups shredded cabbage
1 pound sauerkraut
1/2 pound mushrooms, sliced
2 cooking apples, peeled and sliced
3 tablespoons apricot jam
1 8-ounce can tomato sauce
1 cup beef broth
3/4 cup dry red wine
2 teaspoons salt
1/2 teaspoon freshly ground black pepper
1 clove garlic, minced
1 bay leaf

Melt the butter in a Dutch oven or casserole. Add the onions and pork; cook over medium heat until browned. Add all the remaining ingredients; mix well, cover, and bake in a 325°F. oven for 2 1/2 hours. Taste for seasoning.

Serves 6-8

Koru Ragu
(Swedish Sausage Stew)

A majestic stew that will warm any winter day or even a chilly spring evening.

1-1/2 pounds old fashioned pork
sausage (page 25)
3 tablespoons butter
1/2 cup chopped onions
1 tablespoon flour
1 cup beef broth
1 pound potatoes, peeled and cubed
2 cups sliced carrots
1 teaspoon salt
1/2 teaspoon freshly ground black pepper
1 bay leaf

Lightly brown the sausage in a heavy saucepan. Remove and reserve. Pour off the fat. Melt the butter in the saucepan; sauté the onions 5 minutes. Blend in the flour, then stir in the broth until the mixture boils. Add the sausages, potatoes, carrots, salt, pepper, and bay leaf. Bring to a boil, cover, and cook over low heat 20 minutes.

Serves 6-8

Sausage-Stuffed Egg Rolls

Egg rolls are not pasta but the dough and techniques of working with egg rolls are very similar. You can purchase ready-made egg roll skins from the grocery store or use the following recipe for the skins.

Skins:

2/3 cup sifted all-purpose flour
1/3 cup cornstarch
1/4 teaspoon salt
1 egg
3/4 cup (approx.) water

Filling:

1/2 pound ginger sesame
sausage without casings (page 45)
1 cup very finely chopped celery
1 cup very finely shredded cabbage
1 cup finely chopped green onions
1/2 cup finely shredded carrots
1/2 cup finely chopped fresh mushrooms
1/4 cup finely chopped green sweet pepper
2 teaspoons Worcestershire sauce
1 egg
salt
freshly ground black pepper
1 egg white

Sift together the flour, cornstarch, and salt. Blend the egg with a quarter cup of water and gradually add it to the flour mixture. Slowly add more water and beat until the mixture is smooth. Lightly oil a medium-sized skillet over medium heat. Pour about two tablespoons of the batter into the skillet and tip it in all directions to coat the bottom. If you have an electric crepe maker you can accomplish this task very easily by following the directions that came with the appliance. Cook the skins until the edges curl slightly and they are dry on top. Stack them between sheets of waxed paper until you are ready to fill them. Sauté the sausage in a skillet over medium heat until it is lightly browned. Add all the remaining ingredients except the egg white, mix well, and sauté about two minutes to mix the flavors. Remove the mixture from the heat and allow it to cool. To assemble the egg rolls, place about a quarter-cup of the filling in the center of a skin and fold two sides over to the center. Brush the two sides and the two open edges with the egg white and roll up the skin. Carefully place the egg rolls on a baking pan and refrigerate for about two hours. Deep fat fry the egg rolls until they are crisp and golden. Serve with Chinese (hot) mustard. You can make smaller versions of these egg rolls to serve as hors d'oeuvres by using smaller skins and less filling in each.

Serves 4

Piroghi

Piroghi is a Russian dish, filled dumplings made from a raised dough. Meatless varieties of piroghi are traditional with Russians during Lent and other varieties are common year-round. This recipe calls for a sausage filling.

Dough:

1/2 cup lukewarm water
1 1/4 ounce package dry yeast
2-1/2 cups sifted all-purpose flour
1 egg, well beaten
2 tablespoons rendered chicken fat
or vegetable oil

Filling:

1 pound pork satay sausage removed
from the casing (page 43)
1 small onion, chopped
1 egg, well beaten
Chicken broth or water for boiling
Melted butter
Chopped parsley
salt to taste
freshly ground black pepper

Mix the yeast with one-half cup of lukewarm water and let it rest for fifteen minutes or until it becomes frothy. Add the yeast to the flour with the remaining dough ingredients and mix to make a soft dough. Add a little more water if necessary. Place the dough in a greased bowl and cover. Put the bowl in a warm place to allow the dough to rise. It should double in size. Punch down the dough and roll it out on a floured surface until it is about an eighth of an inch thick. Cut it into circles about three inches in diameter. Sauté the sausage meat until it is lightly browned. Remove it with a slotted spoon and set aside. In the sausage drippings sauté the onion until it is tender. Mix the sausage, onion, and the beaten egg until thoroughly blended. Place about one tablespoon of the sausage mixture on each circle of dough and fold over to form half-moons. Pinch the edges tightly to seal. Place the piroghi, a few at a time, into a large pot of rapidly boiling broth or water and boil for three to four minutes. When all the piroghi are done put them in a large bowl and toss them with butter, parsley, salt and pepper, and serve warm.

Serves 4-6

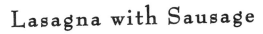

Lasagna with Sausage

If there ever were a party dish for a crowd, lasagna is it. You don't need a special occasion to enjoy this meal, however, and neither do you need a crowd to help you polish it off. Leftover lasagna freezes very well, and if you cut it into serving portions first you can pop it out of the freezer and into the oven and there it is — an instant Italian feast.

2 tablespoons olive oil
1 pound hot or sweet
Italian sausage (page 28)
8 cups tomato sauce
3 eggs, well beaten
1 large (46 oz.) container ricotta cheese
1/4 cup chopped parsley
salt
freshly ground black pepper
1 pound lasagna noodles
1 twelve-ounce package mozzarella cheese
1 cup grated Parmesan cheese
1 cup grated Romano cheese

In a large, deep skillet or a Dutch oven heat the olive oil and brown the sausage. Pour off all but two tablespoons of the drippings. Add the tomato sauce and bring to a simmer. Bring a large pot of salted water to a boil. In a large mixing bowl combine the eggs, ricotta cheese, parsley, salt and black pepper to taste. In the pot of water, cook the lasagna noodles al dente. Drain thoroughly. In a lasagna pan or large baking pan, spread a thin layer of the simmering tomato sauce. Add a layer of lasagna noodles. Spread some of the ricotta mixture over the noodles. Sprinkle about a quarter of the mozzarella, Parmesan, and Romano cheeses over the ricotta. Add a layer of sauce and continue layering in the same fashion until all the ingredients except the sauce are used. Reserve the leftover sauce to pass at the table. End with a layer of sauce. Bake, covered, in a pre-heated 425°F. oven for thirty-five minutes or until the lasagna is bubbly. Test the center with your finger; if it is hot to the touch the lasagna is done.

Note: Lasagna can be prepared several days in advance and stored in the refrigerator. Like a good homemade stew it improves with age.

Serves 10-12

Baked Italian Sausage Crepes

This recipe is very similar to an Italian dish called Baked Stuffed Manicotti which is large tubular pieces of pasta stuffed with various fillings.

16 crepes (page 155)
1-1/2 pounds hot or sweet
Italian turkey sausage
cut into 1/2-inch slices (page 101)
1 small onion, chopped
3/4 pound fresh mushrooms, chopped
8 ounces mozzarella cheese, shredded
2 eggs, well beaten
1 egg, beaten
4 cups basic tomato sauce
1/4 cup grated Parmesan cheese
salt
freshly ground black pepper
chopped fresh parsley to garnish

Prepare the crepes according to the basic recipe and set aside. Sauté the sausage until it is lightly browned, about ten minutes. Remove it to a mixing bowl with a slotted spoon. Sauté the onions and mushrooms in the sausage drippings until the onion is translucent, about ten minutes. Remove with a slotted spoon to the bowl with the sausage. Add the mozzarella and two beaten eggs to the sausage mixture and mix through well. Brush each crepe with the remaining beaten egg. Divide the sausage mixture among the crepes. Place the filling on half of the crepes only and leave a one-inch border. Fold the bare half of each crepe over the filling and press the edges down firmly. Spread half of the tomato sauce in the bottom of a baking pan. Carefully place the crepes in a single layer on top of the sauce. Pour the rest of the sauce over the crepes and sprinkle the Parmesan cheese and parsley evenly over all. Bake in a pre-heated 400°F. oven, covered, for about thirty minutes or until the sauce is bubbly and the crepes are heated through.

Serves 4

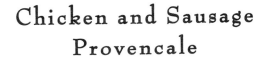

Chicken and Sausage Provencale

Provencale means "in the style of Provence," a geographical and political region of France. In cooking terms, provencale usually means lots of garlic, parsley, and white wine. This recipe is no exception.

2 tablespoons olive oil
1 pound French cervelat sausage (page 49)
2 tablespoons clarified butter
1 three-pound broiler-fryer chicken, cut into serving pieces
1/2 cup flour
3 cloves of garlic, finely minced
4 shallots, finely minced
1 cup dry white wine
1/2 cup chopped parsley
1/2 cup fine bread crumbs
salt
freshly ground black pepper

Heat the olive oil in a large skillet and brown the sausages, about twenty minutes. Place the sausages on a platter and keep them warm. Add the clarified butter to the oil and drippings. Dredge the chicken parts in the flour and sauté them over medium-high heat until they are golden brown, about twenty minutes. Remove the chicken from the skillet and arrange it on the platter with the sausages. Drain off all but two tablespoons of the pan drippings. Add the garlic and shallots and sauté them until they are lightly golden. Be careful not to burn them because burned garlic is extremely bitter. Add the wine and parsley to the skillet and reduce the liquid by half over medium high heat. Scrape the pan to get all the little brown bits clinging to the bottom. Pour the juices over the chicken, coating everything evenly. Add salt and pepper to taste. Sprinkle the bread crumbs over all and place the platter in a pre-heated broiler for about ten minutes until the meat is crisp and the juices are bubbling. Use a lower rack in the broiler to assure that the meat is cooked through before it gets overdone on the outside.

Serves 6-8

Sausage Paprikash

Paprikash means "made with paprika" — usually lots of it. Unfortunately the paprika to which most Americans are accustomed is nothing at all like the real thing. Hungarian paprika comes in a spectrum of flavors ranging from mild and sweet to extremely pungent. One thing that all Hungarian varieties have in common and the thing that most American varieties lack, is flavor. Many people, therefore, think of paprika basically as a coloring agent when it should be a flavoring agent.

2 tablespoons clarified butter
2 pounds Boudin Blanc sausage
cut into one-inch pieces (page 82)
2 large sweet onions, peeled,
quartered, and thinly sliced
4 cups beef or veal stock
1 twelve-ounce can beer or ale
3 tablespoons paprika
1/2 cup chopped parsley
salt
freshly ground black pepper
1 pound egg noodles
3 tablespoons butter or margarine

Heat the butter in a Dutch oven and sauté the sausage until browned. Meanwhile cook noodles according to the package instructions. Add the onion, stock, beer, and paprika. Simmer, uncovered, for thirty minutes. Add the parsley and over medium high heat slowly add the flour until the mixture thickens. Stir constantly. Add salt and pepper.

Drain noodles and stir in butter or margarine. Serve sausage over the noodles along with a hearty imported beer.

Serves 4

Italian Sausage Soup

One of the glories of Italian cooking lies in its combination of simplicity with intense flavors. Richly spiced sausages, powerful cheeses, and fresh vegetables and herbs are often combined with beans, pasta, or rice to provide dishes that are simple and healthy, yet full of flavor. In this delicious soup most of the flavor comes from the sausage.

1 tablespoon olive oil
1 pound Italian Turkey sausage
with sun-dried tomatoes (page 102)
3 cups diced onions
2 quarts beef stock, preferably homemade
1 cup uncooked rice
2 cups chopped fresh or canned Italian-style
tomatoes, drained
salt
freshly ground black pepper to taste
2 cups freshly grated Parmesan cheese
Chopped fresh parsley for garnish

Heat the olive oil in a heavy soup pot. Put in the sausage and cook over medium heat for 4 to 5 minutes, breaking it up as it cooks. Remove the sausage with a slotted spoon and set aside. Add the onions to the fat in the pot and cook over medium heat until totally translucent, about 10 minutes. Add the beef stock, rice, and tomatoes.

Bring to a boil, reduce heat, and simmer, for 20 to 25 minutes or until the rice is tender. Return the sausage to the pot and cook for 5 minutes more. Taste for salt and pepper. Ladle the soup into bowls and sprinkle with lots of Parmesan cheese and a little parsley.

Serves 6

Walnut and Sausage Cake

This cake is similar to those that can be bought along the streets in Berlin, Munich, Frankfurt and other German cities. The sweetness of the icing makes it a good choice for dessert. Without icing, it makes a delicious first course. Or a second one, if you are having soup or salad first.

1 pound bourbon and brown sugar pork sausage, removed from casing (page 42)
1 cup seedless raisins
1 pint boiling water
1 pound brown sugar
1 cup molasses
1 teaspoon cinnamon
1 teaspoon ground cloves
1 teaspoon baking powder
1 cup shelled English walnuts
4 cups all-purpose flour

Combine sausage and raisins. Pour boiling water over mixture and add brown sugar and molasses. Dissolve cinnamon, ground cloves and baking powder in 1–2 tablespoons hot water then add to mixture. Add walnuts. Gradually add flour (add 1 tablespoonful of flour if mixture is not holding together well).

Mix well and pour into a tube pan. Bake in 250°F oven for 1-1/2 hours. While cake is

baking prepare icing. Ice cake while still hot and set aside to cool.

Icing

1 cup confectioner's sugar
3 ounces cream cheese
1-1/2 tablespoons cream or milk
1 teaspoon vanilla
1/2 teaspoon cinnamon

Mix sugar and cream cheese. Gradually beat in cream. Add vanilla and cinnamon mixing well.

Serves 8

Appetizers

SAUSAGE CASINGS
AND HORNS

The edible collagen casings that come with the Popeil Pasta and Sausage Maker are the best for your sausage creations. They're easy to use, store easily and are available in a variety of sizes.

Standard Sausage Casings and Horns

These 3 horns and a supply of casings come with every machine

#20
Breakfast
1 lb. of meat
mixture makes
about 13
4-inch sausages

#26
Italian
1 lb. of meat
mixture makes
about 10
4-inch sausages

#29
Bratwurst
1 lb. of meat
mixture makes
about 9
4-inch sausages

Additional Sizes

#17
Sm. Breakfast
1 lb. of meat
mixture makes
about 15
4-inch sausages

#32
Lg. Bratwurst
1 lb. of meat
mixture makes
about 8
4-inch sausages

Call 1-800-795-2512
to order sausage casings, seasonings and more.

Barbecued Sausage Balls

Barbecued sausage balls are especially good, and are easy to make.

Balls:
1 pound cheesy chuck sausage
removed from casings (page 61)
1 egg, beaten
salt and freshly ground black pepper to taste
1/3 cup bread crumbs

Sauce:
1/2 cup ketchup
salt and freshly ground black pepper to taste
2 tablespoons brown sugar
1 tablespoon vinegar
1 tablespoon soy sauce

Mix all meatball ingredients thoroughly. The mixture should be shaped into balls about one-and-one-half inches in diameter, and these small balls then should be browned slowly in an ungreased skillet for about fifteen minutes. While they are cooking, make the sauce. Serve warm.

Serves 8-10

Sausage-Stuffed Tomatoes

Choose small (but not cherry) tomatoes for this recipe or it may be too filling for an appetizer.

8 small tomatoes
1/2 pound cheesy
chicken sausage (page 122)
1-1/4 cup chopped onion
1/4 cup chopped sweet pepper
1 clove garlic, minced
1 egg, well beaten
dry bread crumbs
salt
freshly ground black pepper
butter or olive oil

Cut a small slice off the stem end of each tomato and remove the seeds and pulp. Be careful not to cut through the walls of the tomatoes. Sprinkle a little salt on each tomato, turn upside down on paper towels and allow to sit for about half an hour. Reserve the pulp. Crumble the sausage in a skillet and sauté over medium heat until lightly browned, about ten minutes. Remove the meat with a slotted spoon and set it aside. Sauté the onion, pepper, and garlic in the sausage drippings until they are crisp-tender, about five minutes. Remove them with a slotted spoon. Combine the sausage, onions, peppers, and garlic with an equal amount of bread crumbs, the egg and about one-half cup of the reserved pulp. Blend the mixture thoroughly. Stuff the tomatoes with the sausage mixture and place on a greased cookie sheet. Dot each tomato with the butter or olive oil. Bake in a pre-heated 400°F. oven fifteen minutes or until the tops are browned.

Serves 8

Guacamole Dip with Chorizos

Guacamole doesn't usually have meat in it but this version is an excellent vehicle for showing off your homemade chorizos.

1/2 pound Mexican chorizo sausage cut into small bite-sized pieces (page 37)
2 large, ripe avocados
1 medium tomato, cored, peeled, seeded, and finely diced
2 cloves garlic, finely minced
1/2 cup mayonnaise
dash hot pepper sauce
1 teaspoon lemon juice
salt
freshly ground black pepper

Sauté the sausages lightly about twenty minutes. Peel the avocado and cut it in half to remove the pit. Mash the avocado in a bowl, using the back of a fork. A food processor would simplify things here. Mash or process the avocados until you get a smooth, pureed consistency. Core, peel, seed, and chop the tomato. Add it to the bowl with the avocado. Mix in the chorizo sausage, garlic, mayonnaise, lemon juice, hot pepper sauce, salt, and pepper. Serve chilled with corn chips

Serves 8.

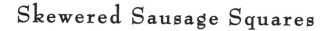

Skewered Sausage Squares

This is a variation on the shish kebab theme. Any hard or semi-hard homemade sausage works well in this recipe, so tailor it to what you have on hand or have a taste for.

1/2 pound American beef sausage cut into
half-inch cubes and browned (page 59)
1/2 pound Swiss or mozzarella
cheese cut into half-inch cubes
1/2 stick butter or margarine
1 teaspoon lemon juice
1 teaspoon paprika
dash of cayenne
toothpicks (approximately 20)

Alternate cubes of sausage and cheese on the toothpicks. About two of each should do it depending on the length of your toothpicks. Melt the butter in a medium-sized skillet and add the lemon juice, paprika, and cayenne. Sauté the skewers gently until the cheese gets soft but does not melt. Serve warm on a heated platter.

Serves 8-10

Sweet and Sour Sausage Spears

Ginger sesame pork sausage (page 45), homemade kielbasa (page 80) and chicken pesto sausage (page 125) make a good combination for this recipe. For an interesting variation soak the skewers in slightly sweet wine or your favorite liqueur in the refrigerator overnight.

1/2 pound cooked sausage of your choice,
cut into half-inch cubes
pineapple cubes
pickled beets, cubed
toothpicks

Arrange alternating pieces of meat, pineapple, and beets on toothpicks and serve well chilled.

Serves 8-10

Texas–Style Barbecue Sausage

Here's another elegant way to serve the lowly Old Fashioned Pork Sausage.

*1 pound old fashioned
pork sausage (page 25)
2 tablespoons vegetable oil
1 16-ounce can tomato sauce (or use
spaghetti sauce)
1 small onion, chopped
1 clove garlic, minced
1/4 cup brown sugar
1/4 cup cider vinegar
1 tablespoon Worcestershire sauce
1 teaspoon Tabasco sauce
1/2 teaspoon celery seed
1 teaspoon dry mustard
1 teaspoon freshly ground white pepper
1/2 teaspoon finely ground coriander
salt to taste*

Cut the sausage into one-inch pieces and sauté in the oil until browned. Combine the remaining ingredients and pour over the sausage. Simmer gently for about ten minutes. Serve in a chafing dish with toothpicks for servers.

Serves 10-12

Broiled Sausage and Mozzarella Mini-Submarine Sandwich

A whole sandwich is more than enough for a meal for one person, but if you cut it up into about eight pieces you'll have tasty appetizers.

1 submarine sandwich roll about twelve inches long (or use a loaf of French bread cut to size)
3/4 pound meatloaf sausage (page 86)
4 ounces shredded mozzarella cheese

Parboil the sausage over medium heat for about twenty minutes with enough water to barely cover the bottom of a skillet. Increase the heat and brown the sausage lightly, about five minutes. Cut the sausage lengthwise almost but not quite all the way through and spread it out flat. Cut the sub roll in the same manner as the sausage and place the sausage in the center of the roll. Sprinkle the mozzarella cheese evenly over the sausage and place the sub, open side up, in a preheated broiler for two or three minutes or just until the cheese is melted. Remove from the broiler, close the sandwich, and cut into serving pieces while still warm.

Serves 8 as an appetizer.

Salami Snacks

Salami slices make a good substitute for crackers. Use your imagination to invent your own toppings.

> *1/2 pound fresh calabrese salami ,*
> *thinly sliced (page 30)*
> *Dijon-style mustard*
> *chopped parsley*
> *carrots cut into short julienne strips*
> *celery cut into short julienne strips*

Lightly broil salami slices until they are thoroughly cooked. Spread each slice with a coating of mustard, sprinkle with parsley and place several strips of carrot and celery on top of each. Arrange on a platter and serve.

Serves 6-8

Sausage Wraparounds

This is hardly a new idea as far as appetizers go but try it with your homemade sausage and see if it doesn't make a whopping difference.

1 pound South African
sausage, browned (page 83)
Swiss or Cheddar cheese
Bacon
Toothpicks

Cut the sausage lengthwise without cutting all the way through. Cut the cheese into sticks and put one in each piece of sausage. Wrap each sausage with a slice of bacon and secure with a toothpick. Broil until the cheese melts and the bacon is crisp. Cut into one-inch chunks and serve warm.

Serves 10-12

Mashed Potato Sausage Balls

The sausage is on the inside in this dish.

1 pound country farm
sausage with casings removed (page 27)
3 cups mashed potatoes
2 eggs, well beaten
2 tablespoons water
1 cup dry bread crumbs
2 tablespoons grated Parmesan cheese
1/2 teaspoon basil
1/2 teaspoon oregano
1 tablespoon parsley, chopped
1 teaspoon finely ground white pepper
dash of cayenne (optional)

Form the sausage meat into small balls. Coat each ball with mashed potatoes. This is a rather tedious procedure. It will help if the potatoes are slightly stiff. Make a wash with the eggs and water. Combine the bread crumbs with the remaining ingredients. Dip each ball into the egg wash and then gently roll it in the seasoned bread crumbs. Place the balls on a baking sheet and let them rest for an hour or so to allow the crumb coating to set. Deep fat fry the balls at about 375°F. until they are golden. Serve hot.

Serves 8-10

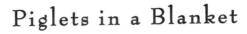

Piglets in a Blanket

What looks like miniature bread loaves on the outside actually hide a real treat on the inside. If you use chorizos with this recipe you'd best play fair and warn your guests before they bite into a piglet or else have a bucket of water handy to put out the flames.

1 pound Mexican chorizo
sausage (page 37)
1 recipe pizza dough

Parboil the sausages in just enough water to cover the bottom of the skillet until they are cooked through, about twenty-five minutes over medium heat. Drain off the liquid and brown the sausages lightly. Divide the pizza dough into as many equal pieces as you have sausage links. Roll out each piece into a square. Place a sausage on one end of each square and roll up the dough. Press to seal the edges. Place the piglets on a greased cookie sheet and bake in a preheated 375°F. oven for about twenty minutes or until the dough is golden brown. Serve warm.

Serves 4-6

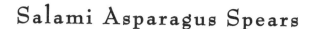

Salami Asparagus Spears

This is a great way to announce the arrival of spring. When those first tender shoots of asparagus poke their heads through the chilly soil you know that spring is just around the corner.

Asparagus spears, small
1/2 pound fresh calabrese salami
sliced into 1-inch lengths (page 30)
Aioli Sauce*
toothpicks

Cook sausage in a frying pan, place on paper towel and refrigerate for one hour. Wash and trim the asparagus under cold running water. Trim off the bottom ends of each spear then cut all the spears into uniform in lengths about 2-inches long. Steam until crisp-tender. Allow to chill in the refrigerator for at least an hour. Generously spread aioli on each piece of salami. Place an asparagus spear on each sausage piece and secure with a toothpick. Always serve well chilled.

Serves 8-10

*Aioli is a French garlic sauce that can be purchased in the gourmet section of most grocery stores.

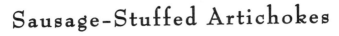

Sausage-Stuffed Artichokes

There are lots of things you can do with artichokes. However, the artichoke is eminently stuffable and makes a visually interesting appetizer.

4 large artichokes
4 bay leaves
4 cloves garlic, crushed
1 lemon, quartered
1 pound country-farm sausage
removed from the casing (page 27)
1/4 cup minced onion
1/4 cup Parmesan cheese
1/2 cup bread crumbs
1 egg, well beaten
1/2 cup dry white wine
1 teaspoon thyme
1 tablespoon chopped capers
pinch of cayenne pepper
salt
freshly ground black pepper
1/2 cup lemon juice
1/4 cup olive oil
2 cloves garlic, finely minced

Prepare the artichokes: Cut off the stem, leaving a flat base. Reserve the stems. Remove any bruised outer leaves. Cut about one inch off the top of each artichoke with a sharp knife. With a pair of kitchen scissors snip off the tip of each outer leaf. Place the artichokes in a pot of boiling salted water along with the bay leaves, four crushed cloves of garlic, and the quartered lemon. Add the stems to the pot and cook, covered, for about half an hour. Remove from water and cool. While the artichokes are bubbling, sauté the sausage in a skillet just until it loses its pink color. Remove the sausage with a slotted spoon and set it aside. In the sausage drippings sauté the minced onion until it is translucent, about ten minutes. In a bowl mix the sausage, onion, Parmesan cheese, bread crumbs, egg, wine, thyme, capers, cayenne, salt, pepper, and, when they are cooked, the artichoke stems, which should be chopped finely. When the artichokes are cooked and cool enough to handle, pull back the leaves and remove the inner choke. Fill the center of each artichoke with equal amounts of stuffing. If you have enough stuffing, place some in between the large leaves at the base. Place the stuffed artichokes in a baking pan and pour the lemon juice mixed with the olive oil and minced garlic over them. Cover and bake in a pre-heated 350°F. oven for about twenty minutes or until the base leaves are very tender. Serve hot with the pan juices for dipping.

Serves 4

Sausage-Stuffed Mushrooms

This hors d'oeuvre is convenient. It looks sophisticated, as if it took a long time to prepare. A half an hour is plenty of time for anyone who knows his way around a kitchen to fix this dish and it may be refrigerated, then re-heated just before guests arrive. To make this recipe work well try to find mushrooms at least an inch and a half in diameter.

18 large mushroom caps
2 tablespoons butter
1/4 pound hot or sweet
Italian sausage (page 28)
2 tablespoons finely minced onions
2 tablespoons butter
1/4 cup dry bread crumbs
2 tablespoons dry sherry
1/2 teaspoon oregano
1 tablespoon fresh parsley, chopped
1 clove garlic, very finely minced
salt
freshly ground black pepper
1/4 pound mozzarella cheese, grated

Wash the mushrooms and remove the stems. Chop the stems finely and set aside. Melt two tablespoons of butter in a large skillet and gently sauté the mushroom caps for two to three minutes or until they are slightly golden, but remove before they are noticeably shrunken. Remove with a slotted spoon and drain on a paper towel. Add sausage and onions to the skillet and sauté for about five minutes, until the meat loses its pink color and the onions are crisp-tender. Remove with a slotted spoon. Add the remaining two tablespoons of butter to the skillet along with the chopped mushroom stems and sauté another two minutes. Remove from heat and add the bread crumbs, sherry, oregano, parsley, garlic, sausage and onion mixture, salt and pepper, and mix well. Add the mozzarella to the mixture and stir. Place an equal amount of the stuffing mixture in each cap. Place the caps on a greased cookie sheet and put in a preheated broiler for two or three minutes or until the cheese bubbles, or refrigerate until needed.

Serves 6-8

Pumpernickel Sausage and Cheese Squares

This hors d'oeuvre is a celebrated crowd pleaser. Fast and easy to make, it is sure to be a hit.

1/2 pound sliced spicy Louisiana sausage,
browned then cut into
one-inch squares (page 93)
1/2 pound sliced Swiss, provolone,
Muenster, or mozzarella cheese,
cut into one-inch squares
7 large pitted black or green
stuffed olives, sliced
5 slices pumpernickel bread, cut
into two-inch squares
toothpicks

Arrange one slice of sausage, one slice of cheese and one slice of olive on each bread square. Secure with a toothpick. Makes about twenty servings.

Serves 8-10

Side Dishes

SAUSAGE CASINGS
AND HORNS

The edible collagen casings that come with the Popeil Pasta and Sausage Maker are the best for your sausage creations. They're easy to use, store easily and are available in a variety of sizes.

Standard Sausage Casings and Horns
These 3 horns and a supply of casings come with every machine

#20
Breakfast
1 lb. of meat mixture makes about 13 4-inch sausages

#26
Italian
1 lb. of meat mixture makes about 10 4-inch sausages

#29
Bratwurst
1 lb. of meat mixture makes about 9 4-inch sausages

Additional Sizes

#17
Sm. Breakfast
1 lb. of meat mixture makes about 15 4-inch sausages

#32
Lg. Bratwurst
1 lb. of meat mixture makes about 8 4-inch sausages

Call 1-800-795-2512
to order sausage casings, seasonings and more.

Sausage and Vegetable Curry

You can use either fresh garlic or chorizo sausages for this recipe or experiment with some other variety.

*3 tablespoons peanut oil
2 pounds French garlic sausage
cut into one-inch pieces (page 55)
1 small onion, chopped
1 carrot, scraped and thinly sliced
4 cups fresh Romano green beans, cut
into one-inch pieces
1 teaspoon red pepper flakes
2 teaspoons (or to taste) curry powder (or
your own blend of coriander, turmeric,
cumin, mace, and pepper)
Buttered rice*

Heat the oil in a large skillet and brown the sausage pieces. Add the onion and carrot and sauté until the carrot is crisp-tender. Add the beans, red pepper, and curry powder, stirring over medium high heat, about ten minutes or until the beans are crisp-tender. Serve over hot buttered rice.

Serves 4

Summer Squash and Sausage

This dish should be seasoned with nothing more than salt and pepper.

2 pounds baby scalloped (pattypan) squash
milk
water
3 tablespoons butter
1 pound old fashioned pork
sausage, browned (page 25)
1 tablespoon flour
salt
freshly ground black pepper

In a pot, boil the baby squash with butter using water and milk in equal amounts, enough to cover squash. Meantime, brown the sausage and remove from pan. Pour off all but about two tablespoonfuls of the sausage grease, then make a roux by adding the flour to the remaining sausage oils and stirring until a light gravy is formed. Return sausage to the pan. When the squash are tender place on top of the sausage, cover and let simmer for 10 minutes. Salt and pepper to taste.

Serves 4

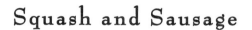

Squash and Sausage

This acorn squash dish can also be done with frankfurters. Go through the same procedure as you would with sausage, slicing one frankfurter into each acorn half. Because frankfurters will need more seasoning than sausage, pour a mixture of honey and melted butter over them, and sprinkle each squash with salt, pepper, and about one-quarter teaspoonful of brown sugar.

2 acorn squash, cut in half and seeded
2 tablespoons melted butter
1/4 cup honey
1/2 pound dried apricot and fresh thyme
chicken sausage (page 121)

Whisk together the honey and melted butter. Pour into the squash shells. The acorn halves should be baked in about one-half inch of water for about a half hour in a 400°F oven with the cut sides up. While the halves are baking, brown sausage in a skillet, turning often as you go, and not allowing them to get too crusty. Spoon sausage in each acorn half. Turn oven down to 325°F, pour more water into the baking pan and place the stuffed squash into the oven. Bake for fifteen minutes. Serve with vegetable of choice.

Serves 4

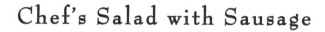

Chef's Salad with Sausage

Most people put bits of chicken, tongue, ham, and sometimes even veal, into a chef's salad, overlooking the delights that sausage can offer. For another twist try spinach, beet greens, watercress or cabbage in place of lettuce.

1 pound chicken pesto sausage (page 125)
1 tablespoon vinegar
1/4 cup olive oil
1 clove garlic, minced
salt
freshly ground black pepper
prepared Dijon mustard
lettuce (iceberg, romaine or endive)
vegetables of choice
cheese of choice
2 hardboiled eggs, diced
3 slices bread, cubed
1 tablespoon butter
Parmesan or ramano cheese, grated

Pan-broil, or pan-fry, sausages and when they are brown, set them into the refrigerator to cool. While the sausages are simmering, make the dressing by mixing vinegar and olive oil. Grind some pepper into this, and add garlic. Salt it lightly, and add some mustard. Bruise everything together with the back of a spoon, then whisk the mixture. Place the bowl containing the dressing in the refrigerator to cool. Put the cooled dressing into a salad bowl and add lettuce and vegetables. Take out the sausages and slice them length-wise or into one half inch pieces. Put them into the vegetable mixture. Now toss the salad lightly, so that each leaf gets coated with the dressing. Set the bowl in the refrigerator. Melt the butter in a frying pan, add bread cubes, allow the cubes to get nearly blackened. Remove the salad bowl again. Add the eggs and toss one more time. Take the fried bread cubes off the stove, drain them on paper or cloth towels, and add them to the salad. Now toss briskly. While you are tossing, sprinkle liberally with grated Parmesan or Romano cheese.

Lima Beans and Sausage

Try this with red wine and black-eyed peas for an interesting twist.

1 16-oz can lima beans
1 pound golden veal lemon
sausage (page 69)
1 onion, shredded
2 tablespoons parsley (fresh or dried)
1/2 cup dry white wine
1/8 cup dry mustard
salt
freshly ground black pepper
1 bay leaf, well ground
2 tomatoes, quartered
1/2 green pepper, slivered
dash Tabasco

Brown sausage. Remove from pan with slotted spoon, saving grease; set aside. Pour beans into a pot and add 1 tablespoon grease from sausage. To the remaining grease in the sausage pan add onion and brown. Add to the beans and sprinkle with parsley. Next lay the sausages over the beans and add dry white wine, mustard, salt, pepper, bay leaf, tomatoes, green peppers and Tabasco. Simmer for 30 minutes.

Serves 4

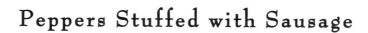

Peppers Stuffed with Sausage

One of the best and easiest ways to make stuffed peppers is with sausages. Try any of your favorite sausages in this recipe for a medley of flavors.

1 pound buttermilk beef sausage (page 62)
4 large green or red peppers
2-1/2 cups bread crumbs
1/4 cup mushrooms, sliced
1/4 cup celery, chopped

Cut off and save tops of peppers; scrape out their seeds. Run some water into each pepper to clean out any seeds that cling. Now fry some loose sausage meat, permitting the grease to remain in the pot or skillet. Add to the sausage the bread crumbs, mushrooms and celery. Mix it all well and use it for stuffing the peppers. Replace the tops and set the stuffed peppers in a pan with about a tablespoon of water. Put the pan in 300°F oven, cook for one and a half hours basting the peppers every 30 minutes.

Serves 2

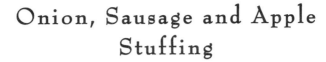

Onion, Sausage and Apple Stuffing

Not only is this stuffing great for turkey, but it makes an enjoyable side dish for ham, chicken, or duck. For a lighter version, bake the stuffing separately in a casserole. That way, it doesn't pick up juice and fat from the roasting bird. Our Apple Chicken sausage makes a delicious,but mild, stuffing. For something a bit spicier, use half Apple Chicken sausage and half Spicy Louisiana Sausage or just Spicy Louisiana Sausage on its own.

2 tablespoons olive oil plus more for casserole
2 pounds apple chicken sausage cut
into bite-sized chunks (page 119)
2 cups chopped onions
1 cup chopped celery
1 tablespoon dried sage
1/4 cup dry white wine or apple cider
8-10 cups dried bread cubes
4 cups peeled, cored, and diced green apples
(such as Granny Smith)
2-3 cups, or more, chicken stock, preferably
homemade
salt
freshly ground black pepper to taste

Preheat the oven to 350°F if baking in a casserole. Heat the oil in a large heavy skillet or

Dutch oven over medium heat. Put in the sausage and fry for 3 minutes. Add the onion, celery, sage, and wine or cider. Cover and cook until the vegetables are soft, stirring occasionally, about 10 minutes. In a large bowl, mix the sausage-vegetable mixture, bread cubes, and apples. Moisten with the stock until the mixture is moist enough to hold together when molded in a large spoon, but not sopping wet. Use more stock if needed. Taste for salt and pepper. At this point you can either stuff the dressing lightly into a turkey or large chicken and roast it following your favorite recipe. Or you can bake the stuffing separately in an oiled casserole. If you cook it in a casserole, stir in a bit more stock to make up for the liquid the stuffing would absorb in the bird. Cover the casserole and bake for 45 minutes. This recipe yields enough stuffing for 1 medium turkey (14 pounds), 2 large roasting chickens (5 to 6 pounds each), 3 frying chickens (3 to 4 pounds each), or 6 to 8 squabs or quail.

Serves 8-10

Wilted Lettuce with Sausage Dressing

This makes a sumptuous lunch. Serve with either pickled beets or tomato slices, salted and peppered, on the side.

1 head iceberg lettuce
1 pound easy chicken
fajita sausage (page 126)
2 tablespoons lemon juice
1/2 teaspoon salt
2 teaspoons sugar

Wash and dry lettuce and cut up into bite-sized pieces. Sauté the sausage in a skillet over low heat for about twelve to fifteen minutes, turning often to make sure it is evenly browned. Remove the sausages from the skillet and drain . Reserve about eight tablespoonfuls of the fat from the sausages and mix it with lemon juice. Add salt and sugar. Put the lettuce pieces into a bowl. Cut up the sausage links into one-inch bits and add to lettuce. Pour the dressing over all, and then toss.

Serves 4

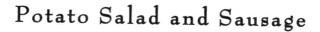

Potato Salad and Sausage

A no-nonsense recipe that you can serve with pride at any meal.

1/2 pound triple mustard pork sausage,
browned and cut into
small pieces (page 39)
2 cups chopped cooked potatoes
1 pickled beet, finely diced
1 teaspoon parsley
1 small onion, grated
mayonnaise

Combine the sausage, potatoes, beet, parsley and onion. This should be mixed with mayonnaise to taste and served on lettuce.

Serves 2

Green Beans and Sausage

In this dish, broccoli or cauliflower could be substituted for the green beans. Serve it with some crusty French bread, the thicker the better.

1-1/2 pounds chicken and ham sausage
with horseradish, cut into
1-inch lengths (page 90)
1 onion, chopped
1 green pepper, chopped
1/2 cup celery, chopped
1-1/2 cups tomatoes, quartered
2 pounds green beans
8 small new potatoes
1/2 cup water

Sauté sausage, onion, pepper and celery until lightly browned. Pour off some of the fat from the sausages. Add tomatoes, green beans, potatoes and water. Cover the pan and simmer for forty-five minutes. Serve hot.

Serves 4-6

Low Fat
One-Dish Meals

SAUSAGE CASINGS
AND HORNS

The edible collagen casings that come with the Popeil Pasta and Sausage Maker are the best for your sausage creations. They're easy to use, store easily and are available in a variety of sizes.

Standard Sausage Casings and Horns

These 3 horns and a supply of casings come with every machine

#20
Breakfast
1 lb. of meat
mixture makes
about 13
4-inch sausages

#26
Italian
1 lb. of meat
mixture makes
about 10
4-inch sausages

#29
Bratwurst
1 lb. of meat
mixture makes
about 9
4-inch sausages

Additional Sizes

#17
Sm. Breakfast
1 lb. of meat
mixture makes
about 15
4-inch sausages

#32
Lg. Bratwurst
1 lb. of meat
mixture makes
about 8
4-inch sausages

Call 1-800-795-2512
to order sausage casings, seasonings and more.

Sausage and Vegetable Hash

This All-American special has been updated so it retains the creaminess of the old-style version, but with fewer calories and much less fat.

3/4 pound red potatoes, diced
1 tablespoon olive oil
1 green bell pepper, diced
1 yellow bell pepper, diced
1 carrot, cut into thin slices
3 scallions, thinly sliced
1/2 pound chicken pesto sausage,
cut into 1/2-inch chunks (page 125)
1/2 teaspoon salt
1/2 teaspoon freshly ground black pepper
1/4 teaspoon dried rosemary
3/4 cup evaporated skimmed milk
3 tablespoons snipped fresh dill

Cook the potatoes until just tender, about 10 minutes. Drain well. In a large skillet, heat the oil until hot but not smoking. Add the bell peppers, carrot, scallions, and potatoes, stirring to coat. Cook until the peppers and carrot are crisp-tender. Stir in sausage, salt, black pepper, and rosemary and cook, stirring frequently, until the sausage is no longer pink, about 5 minutes. Gradually add the evaporated milk and cook, stirring the mixture occasionally, until the hash is nicely crusted and golden brown, about 10 minutes longer. Sprinkle with the dill and serve the hash from pan.

Serves 4

Split Pea Soup with Turkey Sausage

This all-time favorite soup gets its pleasing (and unexpected) reddish-orange color from the sweet potatoes.

1 tablespoon olive oil
1 large onion, finely chopped
4 cloves garlic, minced
2 cloves garlic, halved
2 carrots, thinly sliced
3/4 pound sweet potatoes, peeled
and thinly sliced
1 cup chopped tomato
1 cup green split peas, rinsed
3/4 teaspoon dried thyme
1/4 teaspoon salt
1/4 teaspoon freshly ground black pepper
4 slices (1 ounce each) crusty Italian bread
1/2 pound cooked hot or sweet Italian
turkey sausage, cut into
bite-sized chunks (page 101)
1 tablespoon fresh lemon juice

In a large pot or Dutch oven, heat the oil until hot but not smoking over medium heat. Add the onion and minced garlic and cook, stirring frequently, until the onion has softened, about 5 minutes. Stir in the carrots and sweet potatoes and cook until the carrots and potatoes are softened, about 5 minutes. Add the tomato, stirring to coat. Stir in the split peas, 5 cups of water, the thyme, salt and pepper. Bring to a boil, reduce to a simmer, and cover. Cook, stirring occasionally, until the split peas are tender, about 35 minutes.

Meanwhile, preheat the oven to 400°F. Rub both sides of the bread with the cut sides of the halved garlic; discard the garlic. Cut the bread into 1-inch pieces for croutons. Place the bread on a baking sheet and bake for 5 minutes, or until lightly crisped. Set aside.

Transfer the split pea mixture to a food processor and puree until smooth, about 1 minute. Return the puree to the pot, stir in the turkey sausage and lemon juice, and cook, uncovered, just until the turkey sausage is heated through, about 2 minutes longer. Ladle the soup into bowls, sprinkle the croutons on top, and serve.

Serves 4

Sausage and
Sweet Potato Sauté

This homey weeknight supper is enlivened with mango chutney and Dijon mustard, and for a hint of delicate sweetness and texture, wedges of bartlett pears.

1 pound sweet potatoes, peeled
and cut into 1-inch chunks
2 teaspoons olive oil
3/4 cup diced onion
2 bartlett pears, peeled, cored,
and cut into 8 wedges each
3 tablespoons chopped mango chutney
1 tablespoon fresh lemon juice
2 teaspoons Dijon mustard
3 cups broccoli florets
1/2 pound sweet Greek turkey sausage
with orange, cooked and cut
into 1-inch chunks (page 113)

In a large saucepan of boiling water, cook the sweet potatoes until almost tender, about 5 minutes. Drain well and set aside.

Meanwhile, in a large non-stick skillet, heat the oil until hot but not smoking over medium heat. Add the onion and cook, stirring frequently, until the onion is lightly browned, about 5 minutes. Add the pears to the skillet, stirring to coat. Stir in the chutney, 1/4 cup of water, the lemon juice, and mustard. Bring to a boil, reduce to a simmer, cover, and cook until the pears are almost tender, about 5 minutes (cooking time will vary depending on the ripeness of the pears).

Stir in the sweet potatoes and broccoli and cook, uncovered, until the broccoli is tender, about 5 minutes. Stir in the sausage and cook until the sausage is just heated through, about 4 minutes longer.

Serves 4

Shrimp Sausage Platter

This spicy meal is topped off nicely with fat-free toasted pound cake slices layered with fresh fruit and fat-free whipped topping.

1/2 teaspoon freshly ground black pepper
1/2 teaspoon ground ginger
1/2 teaspoon salt
1/8 teaspoon ground allspice
1/8 teaspoon cayenne pepper
1-1/2 pounds scampi sausage,
lightly browned and
cut into 1-inch chunks (page 136)
2 teaspoons olive oil
1/2 cup minced scallions
4 cloves garlic, slivered
1 tablespoon minced fresh ginger
3/4 pound new potatoes, whole
1 red bell pepper, cut into 1/2-inch cubes
1 cup fat-free chicken broth
1 yellow summer squash, halved lengthwise,
and cut into 1/2-inch thick slices
2 teaspoons cornstarch
2 tablespoons fresh lime juice

In a large bowl, combine the black pepper, ground ginger, salt, allspice and cayenne and stir to blend. Add the sausage, rubbing in the spices until well coated. Set aside. Spray a large non-stick skillet with no-fat cooking spray, add the oil, and heat until hot but not smoking over medium heat. Add the scallions, garlic, and fresh ginger and bell pepper and cook, stirring frequently, until the pepper is crisp-tender, about 4 minutes. Stir in the broth and potatoes, then bring to a boil. Reduce to a simmer, cover, and cook until the potatoes are tender, about 15 more minutes. Stir in the cucumber and sausage, cover again and cook for about 3 minutes.

In a cup, combine the cornstarch and 1 tablespoon of water and stir to blend. Bring the sausage mixture to a boil over medium-high heat, stir in the cornstarch mixture along with the lime juice, and cook, stirring constantly, until the mixture is slightly thickened and the sausage is heated through, about 1 minute longer. Spoon the sausage and vegetables onto a platter and serve.

Serves 4

Stir-Fried Sausage and Vegetables with Orzo

Here orzo, a rice-shaped pasta often found in Greek cooking, absorbs the Asian flavors of the sesame oil and ginger for a wonderful new taste. Serve with pear halves coated with honey and broiled, then topped with toasted, chopped almonds.

1-1/4 cups orzo
2 tablespoons flour
1 pound Asian fish sausage, cut into 1-inch strips (page 140)
2 teaspoons dark Oriental sesame oil
1/2 pound mushrooms, quartered
1 carrot, cut into matchsticks
3 cloves garlic, minced
1 tablespoon minced fresh ginger
3 cups diced Napa cabbage
1 cup halved cherry tomatoes
1/2 cup reduced-sodium soy sauce
1/4 teaspoon firmly packed brown sugar
1/4 teaspoon red pepper flakes
2 teaspoons cornstarch

In a large saucepan of boiling water, cook the orzo until just tender. Drain well and set aside. Meanwhile, on a sheet of waxed paper, spread the flour. Dredge the sausage in the flour, shaking off the excess. In a large non-stick wok or skillet, heat the oil until hot but not smoking over medium heat. Add the sausage and cook, stirring frequently, until browned, about 4 minutes. With a slotted spoon, transfer the sausage to a plate and set aside.

Add the mushrooms, carrot, garlic, and ginger to the pan, stirring to coat. Cook stirring frequently, until the carrot is crisp-tender, about 4 minutes. Stir in the cabbage, cherry tomatoes, broth, soy sauce, brown sugar, and red pepper flakes. Increase the heat to medium-high and bring to a boil.

In a cup, combine the cornstarch and 1 teaspoon of water, stir to blend, and stir into the boiling vegetable mixture along with the orzo. Cook, stirring constantly, until the mixture is slightly thickened, about 2 minutes. Return the sausage to the pan and cook until the sausage is heated through, about 1 minute longer.

Serves 4

Couscous with Sausage
and Vegetables

This simple dish, which is a snap to prepare, will fill the kitchen with the aroma of sweet spices.

2 teaspoons olive oil
1 large onion, diced
4 cloves garlic, minced
2 carrots, cut into 1/2-inch thick slices
1/2 pound apple chicken sausage (page 119)
1 teaspoon curry powder
1/2 teaspoon ground ginger
1/4 teaspoon cinnamon
1/4 teaspoon salt
1/8 teaspoon cayenne pepper
1/8 teaspoon ground allspice
1/8 teaspoon freshly ground black pepper
1 yellow summer squash, halved lengthwise
and cut into 1/2-inch thick slices
1 zucchini, halved lengthwise and
cut into 1/2-inch thick slices
1 cup no-fat chicken broth
2/3 cup couscous
1/4 cup chopped fresh cilantro

In a large non-stick skillet, heat the oil until hot but not smoking over medium heat. Add the onion and garlic and cook, stirring frequently, until the onion is softened, about 7 minutes. Stir in the carrots and cook, stirring frequently, until the carrots are well coated, about 2 minutes. Add the sausage and cook, stirring frequently, until the sausage is slightly brown, about 4 minutes.

Stir in the curry powder, ginger, cinnamon, salt, cayenne, allspice, and black pepper and cook, stirring constantly, until the mixture is fragrant, about 1 minute. Stir in the yellow squash, zucchini, broth, and 1/2 cup of water and bring to a boil. Add the couscous and cook, stirring frequently, until the liquid is absorbed and the sausage is cooked through, about 7 minutes longer. Stir in the cilantro and serve.

Serves 4

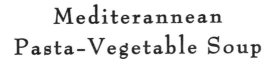

Mediterannean Pasta–Vegetable Soup

Best served with crusty Italian or French bread. Top off with espresso and biscotti.

1 tablespoon olive oil
1 large onion, coarsely chopped
3 cloves garlic, minced
2 carrots, halved lengthwise
and cut into thin slices
5 cups 1/4 inch wide shredded
kale or spinach
2 cups chopped cabbage
2 cups no-fat chicken broth
1 5-1/2 ounce can V-8 juice
1 16-ounce can red kidney beans,
rinsed and drained
5 ounces small elbow macaroni
1/2 teaspoon salt
1/4 cup grated parmesan cheese
1/2 pound Italian turkey sausage with sun-
dried tomatoes, browned and cut into
1/2-inch pieces (page 102)

In a large saucepan or Dutch oven, heat the oil until hot but not smoking over medium heat. Add the onion and garlic and cook, stirring frequently, until the onion has softened, about 5 minutes.

Stir in the carrots, kale, and cabbage and cook, stirring frequently, until the vegetables have softened, about 4 minutes. Stir in the broth, tomato-vegetable juice, and 3 cups of water. Bring to a boil, reduce to a simmer, cover, and cook until the flavors have blended, about 5 minutes.

Uncover the soup, return to a boil over medium heat, and stir in the beans, macaroni, sausage, and salt. Cook, uncovered, until the macaroni is tender, about 8 minutes longer. Remove from the heat and stir in 1 tablespoon of the parmesan. Serve the soup with the remaining 3 tablespoons of parmesan sprinkled on top.

Serves 4

Louisiana Sausage Stew with Dumplings

Sweet molasses, sharp ginger and red wine vinegar give this dish the flavors of the bayou. You can prepare the stew a day ahead and refrigerate it, but wait until re-heating to prepare the lowfat buttermilk dumplings.

1-1/4 cups flour
1/2 teaspoon salt
1/4 teaspoon freshly ground pepper
1 pound easy Cajun turkey sausage,
cut into 3/4-inch chunks (page 107)
1 tablespoon olive oil
1 large onion, cut into chunks
2 cloves garlic, minced
2 cups chopped canned tomatoes,
with their juices
1/2 cup no-fat chicken broth
3 tablespoons red wine vinegar
3 tablespoons molasses
1/2 teaspoon ground ginger
1/2 pound green beans,
cut into 1-inch lengths
3/4 teaspoon baking powder
1/4 teaspoon baking soda
1/8 teaspoon nutmeg
3/4 cup low-fat buttermilk
1 tablespoon chopped parsley

On a sheet of waxed paper, combine 1/4 cup of the flour, 1/4 teaspoon of the salt, and the pepper. Dredge the sausage in the flour mixture, shaking off the excess. In a flameproof casserole or non-stick Dutch oven, heat 2 teaspoons of the oil until hot but not smoking over medium-high heat. Add the sausage and cook until browned, about 4 minutes. With a slotted spoon, transfer the sausage to a plate and set aside. Reduce the heat to medium and add the remaining 1 teaspoon oil to the pan. Add the onion and garlic and cook, stirring frequently, until the onion has softened, about 5 minutes. Stir in the tomatoes with their juices, the broth, vinegar, molasses, and ginger. Bring to a boil, reduce to a simmer, and cook until the liquid is slightly reduced, about 5 minutes. Stir in the beans and cook for 2 minutes.

Meanwhile, in a medium bowl, stir together the remaining 1 cup flour, the baking powder, baking soda, remaining 1/4 teaspoon salt, and nutmeg. Add the buttermilk and parsley and stir until just combined. Return the sausage to the pan, stirring to blend. Return the mixture to a boil, reduce to a simmer, and drop the dumpling mixture by tablespoonfuls onto the simmering stew to make 8 dumplings. Cover and simmer until the dumplings are cooked through, about 10 minutes longer.

Serves 4

Sausage and Mushroom Stew

Simmering the garlic cloves mellows their usual sharpness, while shallots, the most mildly flavored of all the onions, add subtle sweetness and body. As is true of many stews, this one is excellent prepared a day ahead so the flavors can meld.

2 tablespoons flour
1/2 teaspoon salt
1/2 teaspoon freshly ground black pepper
1 pound chicken spinach sausage,
cut into 1-inch chunks (page 128)
2 teaspoons olive oil
8 shallots, peeled
8 cloves garlic, peeled
3/4 pound red potatoes,
cut into 1/2-inch chunks
3/4 pound mushrooms, quartered
2 carrots, thinly sliced
3/4 cup no-fat chicken broth
2 tablespoons fresh lemon juice
1 teaspoon dried tarragon
1-1/4 cups frozen peas
3 scallions, halved lengthwise
and cut into 1-inch lengths
1/4 cup chopped fresh parsley

On a sheet of waxed paper, combine the flour, 1/4 teaspoon of the salt, and 1/4 teaspoon of the pepper. Dredge the sausage in the flour mixture, shaking off the excess. Spray a large saucepan or Dutch oven with non-stick cooking spray, add the oil, and heat until hot but not smoking over medium heat. Add the sausage and cook, stirring frequently, until lightly browned, about 5 minutes.

With a slotted spoon, transfer the sausage to a plate and set aside. Add the shallots and garlic to the pan and cook, shaking the pan frequently, until the mixture is lightly golden, about 2 minutes. Add the potatoes, mushrooms, and carrots, stirring to coat. Stir in the broth, lemon juice, tarragon, remaining 1/4 teaspoon salt, and remaining 1/4 teaspoon pepper. Bring to a boil, reduce to a simmer, cover, and cook until the potatoes and carrots are tender, about 15 minutes.

Return the sausage to the pan along with the peas and scallions and stir well to combine. Simmer, uncovered, until the chicken is cooked through and the peas are hot, about 3 minutes longer. Stir in the parsley and serve.

Serves 4

Sausage Goulash

This variation of the Eastern European classic is filled with chunky vegetables and seasoned in the traditional manner with paprika and caraway seeds. Serve with crusty whole-wheat peasant bread and a fresh fruit platter.

1-1/4 pounds red potatoes,
cut into 1/2-inch chunks
2 teaspoons olive oil
1 large onion, finely chopped
3 cloves garlic, minced
2 carrots, thinly sliced on the diagonal
1/2 pound sweet-sour turkey
sausage (page 114)
1 6-ounce can tomato paste
1/2 cup dry white wine
1 tablespoon paprika
1/2 teaspoon caraway seeds
1/2 teaspoon salt
1/4 teaspoon freshly ground black pepper
2-1/2 cups frozen peas
2 tablespoons no-fat sour cream

In a large saucepan of boiling water, cook the potatoes until tender, about 12 minutes. Drain well and set aside. Meanwhile, in a non-stick Dutch oven, heat the oil until hot but not smoking over medium heat. Add the onion and garlic and cook, stirring frequently, until the onion has softened, about 5 minutes. Stir in the carrots and cook, stirring frequently, until the carrots are tender, about 5 minutes. Add the sausage and cook, stirring frequently, until no longer pink, about 4 minutes.

In a small bowl, combine the tomato paste, 3/4 cup of water, the wine, paprika, caraway seeds, salt, and pepper and stir to blend, then stir into the pan. Bring to a boil, reduce to a simmer, cover, and cook until the sausage is richly flavored, about 10 minutes. Stir in the peas and potatoes, cover again, and cook just until the peas and potatoes are heated through, about 3 minutes longer. Remove from the heat before stirring in the sour cream to avoid curdling. Serve piping hot in large bowls.

Serves 4

Lamb Sausage with Spinach Fusilli

After rinsing and drying fresh dill, use kitchen shears to snip the feathery fronds directly into a measuring cup, avoiding the stems, until you have the amount the recipe calls for.

6 ounces spinach fusilli pasta
1/2 pound lamb sausage
with rosemary, cut into
1-inch chunks (page 71)
3 tablespoons plain low-fat yogurt
1/4 teaspoon salt
1/4 teaspoon freshly ground black pepper
3 tablespoons plain dried
breadcrumbs, crushed
2 teaspoons olive oil
1/3 cup minced scallions
1/4 cup snipped, fresh dill
3 cups cauliflower florets
1 red bell pepper, diced
1 14-1/2 ounce can stewed tomatoes,
chopped with their juices
1/3 cup no-fat chicken broth
2 tablespoons tomato paste

In a large pot of boiling water, cook the fusilli until just tender. Drain well and set aside. Meanwhile, in a medium bowl, coat the sausage chunks with a mix of yogurt, salt and black pepper, then dredge with breadcrumbs. Mix until sausage chunks are well coated. Set aside. In a large skillet, heat the oil until hot but not smoking over medium heat. Add the coated sausage and sauté lightly about 2 minutes until coating is slightly crusty on all sides. Remove and set aside

To the same pan, add the scallions, dill, cauliflower and bell pepper and cook until the cauliflower is lightly golden, about 2 minutes. Stir in the tomatoes with their juices, the broth, and tomato paste, then bring to a boil.

Add the sausage, reduce to a simmer, cover, and cook until the sausage is just cooked through, about 5 minutes. Stir in the fusilli and cook, uncovered, until the fusilli is just heated through, about 3 minutes longer. Divide the sausages, fusilli, and vegetables among 4 bowls and serve.

Serves 4

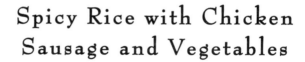

Spicy Rice with Chicken Sausage and Vegetables

For a nuttier taste, substitute basmati or Texmati rice for the long-grain white, and for a more pungent garnish, chopped cilantro instead of parsley. If re-heating leftovers, add a little chicken broth or water beforehand to keep the rice moist.

2 teaspoons olive oil
1/4 cup thinly sliced scallions
3 cloves garlic, minced
1 zucchini, quartered lengthwise
and cut into 1/2 inch thick slices
1 red bell pepper, diced
1-1/4 cups medium-hot prepared fresh salsa
1 tablespoon fresh lime juice
1 cup long-grain rice
2 cups no-fat chicken broth
1/2 teaspoon dried oregano
1/4 teaspoon dried thyme
1/8 teaspoon cayenne pepper
1/2 pound easy chicken fajita sausage,
lightly browned (page 126)
2 tablespoons chopped fresh parsley

In a large skillet, heat the oil until hot but not smoking over medium heat. Add the scallions and garlic and cook, stirring frequently, until the mixture is softened, about 2 minutes. Add the zucchini and bell pepper and cook, stirring frequently, until the pepper is tender, about 5 minutes. Transfer the vegetable mixture to a medium bowl, stir in the salsa and lime juice, and set aside. In the same pan lightly brown your sausage making sure it is cooked evenly on all sides. Remove and set aside. Add the rice to the pan, stirring to coat. Stir in the broth, oregano, thyme, and cayenne. Bring to a boil, reduce to a simmer, cover, and cook until the rice is almost tender and the liquid is absorbed, about 12 minutes.

Return the vegetable mixture to the pan, stir well, and return to a boil over medium-high heat. Reduce to a simmer and return sausage to the pan, cover again, and cook until the rice and sausage are tender, about 9 minutes longer. Remove sausage and stir in the parsley. Arrange the rice with sausage on a large platter top with parsley and serve steaming hot.

Serves 4

Skillet Spaghetti and Sausage

This low calorie dish is best served with garlic toast and, for desert, a fresh fruit salad garnished with no-fat whipped topping.

1/4 pound Romano chicken sausage,
cut into 1-inch chunks (page 124)
1/4 pound hot or sweet Italian turkey
sausage, cut into 1-inch chunks (page 101)
3 tablespoons flour
2 teaspoons olive oil
1 14-1/2 ounce can stewed tomatoes,
chopped with their juices
2 strips orange zest, each about 3 inches long
3/4 cup orange juice, preferably fresh
8 ounces thin spaghetti, broken into thirds
1 cup thinly sliced zucchini
1 cup thinly sliced yellow summer squash
1/2 cup sliced, ripe olives
1/4 cup freshly grated parmesan cheese

On a sheet of waxed paper, spread the flour. Dredge the sausages in the flour, shaking off the excess. In a large non-stick skillet, heat the oil until hot but not smoking over medium heat. Add the sausages, in batches if necessary, and cook until lightly browned, about 3 minutes. Stir in the tomatoes with their juices, 1-1/4 cups of water, the orange zest, orange juice, remaining 1/4 teaspoon thyme, and remaining 1/4 teaspoon sage until well combined. Bring to a boil, reduce to a simmer, cover and cook until the sausages are almost cooked through, about 5 minutes. Increase the heat to medium, return to a boil, and stir in the spaghetti, zucchini, and yellow squash and ripe olives. Cover again and cook, stirring occasionally, until the spaghetti is tender and the sausages are cooked through, about 15 minutes longer. Divide the spaghetti and sausages among 4 bowls, sprinkle with parmesan and serve.

Serves 4

Country-Style
Sausage Fricassee

This old-fashioned favorite is great served with buttermilk biscuits, followed by baked apples topped with raisins, cinnamon and fat-free cream substitute.

1/4 cup flour
1/2 teaspoon salt
4 teaspoons freshly ground black pepper
1 pound apple chicken sausage,
cut into 1-inch pieces (page 119)
2 teaspoons olive oil
1 large onion, finely chopped
1-1/2 cups no-fat chicken broth
1-1/3 cups frozen baby lima beans
or peas, thawed
1 yellow summer squash, halved lengthwise
and cut into 1/2-inch thick slices
8 ounces vermicelli, broken into thirds
2 tablespoons no-fat sour cream
2 tablespoons snipped fresh dill

On a sheet of waxed paper, combine the flour, 1/4 teaspoon of the salt, and the pepper. Dredge the sausage in the flour mixture, shaking off the excess. In a non-stick Dutch oven, heat 1 teaspoon of the oil until hot but not smoking over medium heat. Add the sausage, in batches if necessary, and cook until lightly browned on all sides, about 6 minutes. Transfer the sausage to a plate and set aside. Add the remaining 1 teaspoon oil to the pan. Add the onion and cook, stirring frequently, until the onion has softened, about 5 minutes. Stir in the broth, 1/2 cup of water, and the beans.

Return the sausage to the pan. Bring to a boil over medium-high heat, reduce to a simmer, cover, and cook for 10 minutes. Stir in the squash, vermicelli, and remaining 1/4 teaspoon salt. Return to a boil, reduce to a simmer, and cover again. Cook until the vermicelli is just tender and the sausage is cooked through, about 7 minutes longer. Remove from the heat and stir in the sour cream and dill. Divide the chicken fricassee among bowls and serve.

Serves 4

StirFry Antipasto Dinner

This colorful dish is a quick and easy stir-fry with an Italian flair. Try substituting red wine vinegar for the balsamic.

3/4 pound small red potatoes, quartered
1 9-ounce package frozen artichoke hearts
1 tablespoon extra-virgin olive oil
1 medium red onion, cut into 1-inch chunks
1 red bell pepper, cut into 1 inch pieces
2 ribs celery, halved lengthwise
and cut into 1-inch slices
1 zucchini, cut into 1 by 1/2-inch strips
1-1/4 cups canned garbanzo beans,
rinsed and drained
1/2 pound turkey meatloaf sausage,
lightly browned and cut into
1-inch pieces (page 110)
3 tablespoons balsamic vinegar
1 tablespoon chopped fresh parsley

In a large saucepan of boiling water, cook the potatoes for 10 minutes. Add the artichokes and continue to cook until the potatoes are just tender, abut 5 minutes longer. Drain the potatoes and artichokes well and pat dry with paper towels. Set aside. Meanwhile lightly brown sausage and set aside. In a large non-stick skillet, heat 2 teaspoons of the oil until hot but not smoking over medium heat. Add the onion and bell pepper and cook, stirring frequently, until the pepper is crisp-tender, about 5 minutes. Stir in the potatoes and artichokes and cook, stirring frequently, until the artichokes are tender, about 5 minutes.

Stir in the celery and zucchini and cook, stirring frequently, until the celery and zucchini are crisp-tender, about 3 minutes. Stir in the garbanzos and sausage and cook just until the garbanzos and sausage are heated through, about 3 minutes longer. Gently stir in the remaining 1 teaspoon oil, the vinegar, and parsley. Spoon the antipasto mixture onto plates and serve.

Serves 4

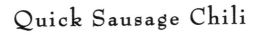

Quick Sausage Chili

For a complete meal, try serving this tasty chili with squares of corn bread, coleslaw made with nonfat mayonnaise, and no-fat chocolate chip cookies.

1 teaspoon olive oil
1 large onion, finely chopped
1 green bell pepper, cut into 3/4-inch chunks
3 cloves garlic, minced
3/4 pound Tex-Mex sweet turkey sausage,
cut into 1/2-inch pieces (page 108)
1 teaspoon mild chili powder
2 teaspoons flour
1 teaspoon ground cumin
3/4 teaspoon dried oregano
2 14-1/2 ounce cans no-salt-added stewed
tomatoes, chopped with their juices
2 tablespoons tomato paste
1/2 teaspoon salt
2 16-ounce cans red kidney beans,
rinsed and drained
1-3/4 cups frozen corn kernels

In a Dutch oven, heat the oil until hot but not smoking over medium heat. Add the onion, bell pepper, and garlic and cook, stirring frequently, until the vegetables are fragrant and softened, about 7 minutes. Add the sausage and cook until no longer pink, about 6 minutes. Stir in the chili

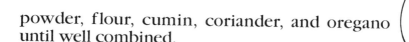

powder, flour, cumin, coriander, and oregano until well combined.

Stir in the tomatoes with their juices, the tomato paste, and salt and cook, stirring frequently, until the sausage is nicely coated and the mixture is slightly thickened, 5 to 7 minutes. Stir in the beans and corn and cook until the vegetables are heated through, about 2 minutes longer.

Serves 4